Critical Guides to French Texts

41 Hugo: Les Contemplations

Critical Guides to French Texts

EDITED BY ROGER LITTLE, WOLFGANG VAN EMDEN, DAVID WILLIAMS

HUGO

Les Contemplations

Peter Cogman

Lecturer in French
University of Southampton

Grant & Cutler Ltd
1984

I.S.B.N. 84-499-7322-8

DEPÓSITO LEGAL: v. 1.357 - 1984

Printed in Spain by
Artes Gráficas Soler, S.A., Valencia
for
GRANT & CUTLER LTD
11 BUCKINGHAM STREET, LONDON W.C.2

Contents

Prefatory Note

References to *Les Contemplations* in the text are to the edition by Pierre Albouy published by Gallimard in the Collection Poésie, in the form I, i, 1, p.33 = Book I, poem i, line 1, p.33 (the last two only when necessary), in order to facilitate reference to other editions. Italicized numbers in parentheses, followed by page references, refer to the numbered items in the select bibliography at the end of this volume. The epigraphs to the chapters are from *William Shakespeare*, Hugo's study of genius and also, obliquely, of himself. For this and Hugo's other writings I have used the chronological *Œuvres complètes* edited by Jean Massin (for details see bibliography item *1*).

P.W.M.C.

Introduction

> 'Aux livres colosses il faut des lecteurs
> athlètes.' (*1*, XII, p.263)

There are two obstacles in the way of an appreciation of Hugo's poetry. The first is Hugo himself. A set image of the poet can easily distort a response to the poetry; it did so even at the time of publication, when a critic felt driven to interpret the erotic encounter of 'Elle était déchaussée' (I, xxi) as an allegory of the union of the poet and democracy since he found it impossible to read literally, alongside 'des vers admirables sur ses filles si pures et si belles' (*4*, I, p.cxvi). But Hugo cannot without oversimplification be reduced to any one of the vivid images that he left, and in part cultivated: affectionate father, inexhaustible lover, obstinate exile, visionary sage, whitebearded grandfather. Even when these obtrusive images have been put to one side, there remains the oceanic bulk and variety of Hugo's production. The reader of later French poetry tends to react to this quantity in terms of misleading oppositions: contrasting unfavourably Hugo's loquacity and eloquence with the brevity and apparent simplicity of a Verlaine, seeing his rhetoric and apparent facility, the element of posing and self-aggrandizement, as the opposite of 'genuine' emotion, and his directness and immediate intelligibility as the opposite of a poetry of difficulty, density, enigmatic charm, suggestion, and mystery: that of Nerval, Baudelaire, or Mallarmé. In its very variety, Hugo's poetry presents an obstacle to the critical instinct to classify. Is *Les Contemplations*, published in 1856, and including poems written as far back as 1834, the last great volume of the first wave of French Romantic poetry, one where the poet tackles the great lyric themes: love, suffering, death, nature, God, and presents himself directly to the reader both as a teacher pinning down the injustices of society, and as a prophet explaining the universe?

No doubt, but at the same time the poems reveal a new Hugo and a new sort of poetry, one that bewildered contemporary critics with a proto-surrealist plunge into a nightmarish dream-world and with the indulgence of exuberant verbal fun, both of which were equally shocking to their conviction that 'la poésie ... doit rester *rationnelle*' (*4*, I, p.cv). There is both continuity and novelty in the volume. It is a product of its time, in terms of its social preoccupations, its aesthetic concerns (the revolution in poetic language and form), its ideas (the revelations of Book VI); but also the volume is bolder, more varied, more rewarding than any of Hugo's previous collections, and is indeed, as he wrote to his publisher, '[son] œuvre de poésie la plus complète' (*1*, IX, p.1090).

I have consequently attempted to examine the effectiveness of the poems, and sometimes their weakness, as embodiments of aspects of Hugo's vision of the world and of man. After a discussion of some general issues, I have tried to illuminate the main areas explored by Hugo, and his response to them; and to examine the varied poetic resources which he exploits, renews, and creates, in order to convey this response to the reader. The categories I use are not watertight, either as regards themes or techniques: Hugo's main preoccupations are related, and he does not reserve any one technique for any one theme. And there remain inevitably poems — such as the miraculous 'Fête chez Thérèse' (I, xxii) — which elude any categorization.

1. The 'I' of the Poet

'Ce sont des hommes surhumains, mais
des hommes. *Homo sum.* Cette parole
d'un poëte résume toute la poésie.' (*I*,
XII, p.263)

Can we attempt to approach *Les Contemplations* with no
'extraneous' knowledge of Hugo the man, and of his times? He
himself referred to the volume as 'poésie pure' (*I*, VIII, p.1033),
by which he meant non-topical poetry, as opposed to the
political satire of *Châtiments*. If we are tempted to do so, we
immediately run into difficulties. The poet himself alludes to his
career, both in literature ('Réponse à un acte d'accusation', I,
vii) and in politics ('Ecrit en 1846', V, iii). The structure of the
volume hinges on the pivotal year 1843, that of the death of his
older daughter, commemorated in Book IV. From the start, the
Preface presents the volume as autobiography, 'les Mémoires
d'une âme'. And as such they are the memoirs of a figure both
distinguished and notorious: a celebrated writer whose private
life had not been free of scandal, whose recent public career had
been heroic, naive, or misguided, depending on one's point of
view.

Who was Victor Hugo for the public of 1856? Born in 1802,
the third son of an officer in Napoleon's armies who was to
finish as a general, his first successes had come as a poet,
securing a royal pension with his *Odes* of 1822, in which he
showed himself a defender of the restored Bourbon monarchy
and the Roman Catholic Church. He continued his poetic career
with the technically virtuosic *Orientales* (1829) and four volumes
of lyric poetry between 1831 and 1840, while at the same time
showing his versatility by establishing rapid pre-eminence in the
fashionable areas of drama and the historical novel. His sense of
the social role of the poet led to concern with social problems

such as capital punishment and the fate of the freed convict, and he moved towards an undoctrinaire commitment to the ideals of the Revolution of 1789: liberty, equality, fraternity, while remaining attached to order and the rights of property. In religion too he moved from traditional forms to a more personal and deeply felt sense of God, becoming overtly hostile to any church; from 1850 he was an independent mystic who could say: 'Je crois à Dieu direct' (see 'Relligio', VI, xx). Though made a peer in 1845, he showed himself lacking in the oratorical and the tactical, practical skills of the politician. What fired his imagination were things with immediate emotional impact that he could *see*: social injustice, the sufferings of the deprived, but without clearly probing their cause — the scenes of 'Melancholia' (III, ii). The Republic established in 1848 on the fall of Louis-Philippe led to an outburst of Hugolian optimism: he foresaw the abolition of poverty, of ignorance, of war. But it also served to detach him from the conservative majority when he saw that they were concerned, not with ideals, but with preserving their position; and from the President, Louis-Napoléon Bonaparte, when it became clear that he was intent on staying in power. Hugo's resistance to his *coup d'état* in 1851 led to flight into exile, first in Belgium, then in the Channel Islands, and to the end of Hugo's political and social career, but also to his re-emergence as a writer. The events of 1848-51 had largely interrupted his literary activity, but exile prompted a pamphlet, *Napoléon le Petit*, and a wave of satirical verse directed against the new Emperor. This invective was collected in a volume, *Châtiments*, and published in Belgium in 1853. The resumption of poetic activity led to the completion of *Les Contemplations*, from which the exclusion of topical political concerns made publication in France possible. The fact of exile is present in it, but not its immediate political causes, not the events of 1848-51.

The facts of Hugo's public career are a mixture of ambition, calculation, independence, and idealism; they resist the schematized view he presents of it in 'Ecrit en 1846' as a sudden conversion: 'J'ai devant moi le jour et j'ai la nuit derrière' (V, iii, 381, p.251). The same could be said of what is misleadingly termed his private life. 'Aux Feuillantines' (V, x) presents memories of a happy childhood, suppressing any reference to the tensions between his parents and the mutual infidelities which led to their legal separation in 1818. A similar pattern was to reappear in Hugo's life: married in 1822, after five successive pregnancies (four children survived) his wife refused to sleep with him, but responded to the less aggressive advances of the writer and critic Sainte-Beuve (1830). Hugo took the actress Juliette Drouet as mistress in 1833, but the family remained together. His wife appears in *Les Contemplations* only as the mother of Léopoldine ('Dolorosae', V, xii), drowned in a boating accident with her husband in 1843, shortly after their marriage; Hugo was on holiday with Juliette Drouet at the time, and, like the public, learned of the accident through the newspaper. The continuity of the liaison with Juliette, who accompanied him into exile, did not preclude numerous other affairs, most notoriously with Léonie Biard, with whom he was discovered *in flagrante delicto* by the law in 1845; the fact that he had just been named a peer saved him from imprisonment. The consequent public shame, with loss of favour at court and hostile allusions in the press, was a blow to his self-esteem as husband and public figure, a first 'exile'. The Hugo of robust health, unflagging energy, and enormous appetite for life, was also dogged by domestic misfortune: the deaths of Léopoldine, of Juliette's daughter Claire Pradier, the madness of his brother Eugène on his own wedding day, later that of his own daughter Adèle, who was interned in 1872.

The fear of madness may play a part in one of the more curious episodes of Hugo's life at the time the volume was taking shape. In September 1853 Mme de Girardin, visiting Hugo in Jersey, had introduced his circle to the latest Parisian fashion, communicating with the spiritual world by table-rapping. Two small tables were superposed, the participants placed their hands on top, and the spirits dictated: one blow for 'a', etc. Hugo, initially sceptical, was gradually convinced of the supernatural character of the revelations and in 1853-55 spent long sessions in these séances, visited by a variety of surprising interlocutors, from Balaam's Ass to Shakespeare. At the same time he wrote an enormous amount of visionary poetry, a small part of which appears in Book VI. When he abandoned the tables, it was for a variety of reasons, including their evasiveness on key questions, his desire to preserve his independence as poet-seer, and the sudden madness and internment of one participant, Jules Allix. The tables were not important as a source; they largely reflected, or as Hugo saw it, endorsed ideas he held already. But they were a crucial stimulus to his creativity, and an encouragement to express fully and systematically his meta-physical preoccupations.

Hugo thought at one moment of acknowledging a debt to the tables for the two details he borrowed from them (*1*, IX, pp.1087, 1432), but no hint of the role of the séances appears in *Les Contemplations*. In general, the history of the composition of the volume, over some ten years, shows Hugo struggling with two main problems: what precisely to include, and how to organize it. Both the omissions about his private life and the simplification in the presentation of his political evolution make it clear that there is no exact equivalence between the experiences and career of Victor Hugo, and the version suggested by *Les Contemplations*. Not that we should criticize him on this account. He is not a confessional poet, revealing the details of his life, but a poet using the material of his life to construct from it a significant and exemplary pattern, one might say a myth. The pattern that he constructs is one that is as generally applicable as possible; hence the claim of the Preface: 'Quand je vous parle de moi, je vous parle de vous'. This claim is stated explicitly in the poems. 'Le poëme éploré se lamente' not only repeats the Romantic view that the poet/dramatist portrays himself in his creatures, and 's'arrachant les entrailles, les met / Dans son drame', i.e. asserts that they are him, but also affirms that he has been them. He has a potential (Keats would say a 'negative capacity') to be more than himself:

> Ce qui fait qu'il est dieu, c'est plus d'humanité.
> Il est génie, étant, plus que les autres, homme.
>
> (I, ix, 24-25, p.52)

Hugo's claim is also implicit in the language of the poems,

perhaps most effectively in the pronouns of 'Ce que c'est que la mort':

> On voit ce que je vois et ce que vous voyez;
> On est l'homme mauvais que je suis, que vous êtes ...
> (VI, xxii)

The poem continues with this insistent *on*, standing for both poet and reader, to the final joyous transformation by death of 'notre être'.

At the centre of *Les Contemplations* is this representative 'I'; if Hugo's wife does not appear in Book IV, it is because she is not relevant to the issues he has to deal with there, namely an individual's response to death; if she does appear in 'Dolorosae', it is because he is in Book V concerned with exile and memories, and with the memory of a loss jointly kept alive in this poem.

One of the clearest signs of the construction of this mythical central 'I' is the way Hugo has manipulated the dates of the poems. The Preface implies that the poems were written as the poet lived: 'Vingt-cinq années sont dans ces deux volumes ... L'auteur a laissé, pour ainsi dire, ce livre se faire en lui'. The final poem repeats the idea: 'J'ai, dans ce livre, enregistré mes jours' (line 147, p.415). But the dates that are printed after the poems — generally a specific year and a month, often with a place as well — are in the majority of cases not the dates which Hugo put at the end of his manuscript. Only in about 40 cases are they the same; in some cases the change is considerable: 'A propos d'Horace' (I, xiii), completed in 1855, is dated 'mai 1831' in the volume.

Before we start detaching and shuffling the pages of the volume, in quest of an elusive 'real Hugo',[1] we should bear in mind the various reasons for these 'falsifications'. The least important, though none the less real, is biographical circumstance: concern for others may have led Hugo to conceal from the public that the erotic escapade of I, xxi was composed in

---

[1] Even the MS dates can mislead, as they show the date of *completion* of the final fair copy, and some poems were composed over several years.

1853 in the supposed austerity of exile, or to conceal from his family that the first poem in Jersey (V, xxiv) was for Juliette Drouet. A second possibility is that the date (or place) given to the poem is a pointer to its significance in the same way that a title can be. In Book IV, the date of Léopoldine's death (4 September 1843) is given between poems ii and iii; iii is called 'Trois ans après' and dated 'novembre 1846'; other poems (notably xiv and xv) are presented, by their dates, as successive commemorations of Léopoldine's death, stages in his reaction to it. Other dates and places may have a purely private commemorative value for the poet too: 'I remember, I was there then', but this is not always accessible to the reader.

The third, most fundamental, reason is plausibility. Incidents and experiences are fitted into a conventional mould to make them more immediately assimilable to 'l'histoire de tous'. A poem written about the spring in October (I, xii) is redated 'mai'; it is whimsical and carefree, so the year is changed from 1854 to 1831, and it finds its place in Book I. Conversely the cheerless nature of V, vi is redated from May to January. 'Le poète s'en va dans les champs' (I, ii), the first poem to be completed after Léopoldine's death, is put back to June 1831, since in the volume the poet cannot 'regarder les fleurs qui sont dans le gazon' (IV, xv, 12, p.227) until four years after her death. Hugo, in his life, did; if we ask why he did so, we are being sidetracked into psychological explanation (it is, for example, a defence mechanism against grief), rather than seeing the pattern that Hugo is creating. In reality, Hugo's temperament oscillated between moments of joy and sombre visions: the gay I, xii was completed the day after finishing the apocalyptic 'Ce que dit la bouche d'ombre'.[2] In the volume, joy precedes terror, conforming to the conventional movement from carefree youth to meditative old age. Out of a paradoxical personal psychological fact, Hugo constructs a mythic itinerary.

Hugo's temperamental oscillation, in the face of the universe, between joy and terror, is one manifestation of a tendency to

[2] Other factors can lie behind such coincidences. The range of poems completed in 1854, after Hugo had concluded a contract with his publisher Hetzel, springs *also* from the increasingly clear structural demands of the volume.

explore a theme in terms of opposite responses that are complementary, i.e. both parts of the same whole, rather than mutually exclusive, indeed to intensify these oppositions as much as possible. 'Les qualités les plus diverses, les plus complexes, les plus opposées en apparence, entrent dans la composition des âmes. Les contraires ne s'excluent pas; loin de là, ils se complètent' (*I*, XII, p.222). What is true of the individual is true also of man, who is body and soul, reason and intuition; it is true of the world, grotesque and sublime, in the terms that Hugo uses in his first major literary manifesto, the Preface to *Cromwell*. Hugo wishes to encompass both poles, to express the totality of life, but also tends to perceive and respond to things in terms of their opposed components, seeing the world in terms of a traditional dualism which goes back in France to Descartes, one that opposes mind and body, and in terms of an even older manichean opposition between spirit and matter, good and evil. This clearly corresponds to his imagination's tendency to perceive things in terms of contrasting oppositions: light and dark, great and small, and gives these oppositions a strength that comes from their roots both in his artistic sensibility and in his ideas. But what Hugo looked forward to philosophically and religiously was a final reconciliation between the two terms; what he seeks artistically is to comprehend both in an overall unity. In 'La source tombait du rocher' (V, iv) ocean and spring represent a harmonious complementarity, two equally necessary aspects of the world: great and small, strong and weak.

In consequence individual poems may appear to show contradictions and inconsistencies, but these should be seen as the contrasting facets of one truth, in the same way that melancholy and *fantaisie* are 'l'un [et] l'autre versant du rêve' (*I*, XII, p.464). Thus with religion: at times God is seen as immanent, permanently pervading the universe which receives 'la pénétration de la sève sacrée' ('Eclaircie', VI, x), and participating in all aspects of nature, through which he can be sensed (though Hugo resists the pantheist temptation to identify nature with God). At other times God is seen as transcendent, beyond nature:

L'hosanna des forêts, des fleuves et des plaines,
S'élève gravement vers Dieu, père du jour.

                                        (I, iv, 24-25, p.37)

All nature comes together to celebrate God, but does not reach
Him; and Hugo can emphasize the inaccessibility of a God who
created the universe and its inexorable laws. This God is often
felt of as a person, but He is remote from man, apparently
incomprehensible, even cruel. This is the God addressed in 'A
Villequier' (IV, xv).

There is the same polarization with love. At times Hugo
expresses the conviction that love, even the sensual love of Book
II, is innocent, and that it is approved of and encouraged by all
nature. In 'Premier mai' (II, i), 'Tout conjugue le verbe aimer';
in 'Crépuscule', even 'Dieu veut qu'on ait aimé' (II, xxvi). At
other times, love is seen as spiritual and eternal, and clearly
distinguished from sensual pleasure (V, xx), which is not truly
love but an enslavement and degradation of 'l'âme' by 'notre
chair coupable' (VI, viii, 93-94, p.332).

Any 'real Hugo' must remain elusive, any attempt to catch
him out in self-contradiction is vain. It is from the multiple
aspects of himself and the world that he constructs his poems,
and constructs the 'self' that evolves in the course of *Les
Contemplations*. It cannot be denied that this mythical
treatment of the self entails a great deal of striking of attitudes,
notably in Books V and VI: Hugo the Exile, Hugo the Seer. This
is achieved partly by a transformation of the setting. In 'A vous
qui êtes là', the Jersey shore becomes bleak, barren, hostile (one
might almost think no one lived there):

Sur cette grève nue, aigre, isolée et vide,
Où l'on ne voit qu'espace âpre et silencieux,
Solitude sur terre et solitude aux cieux;

                                        (V, vi, 6-8, p.258)

It is compared successively to night, a *bagne*, an eclipse, and a
coffin. If Hugo makes it visited by 'l'aigle qui fuit les hommes
importuns', the eagle is there not for the sake of realism, but as a

symbol of proud independence. In this poem the exiled poet
appears in the third person: 'l'être mystérieux qu'un vent fatal
emporte'. Elsewhere he is transformed in various ways. He is set
in parallel to Socrates, Jesus, and Galileo: he is, like them, a
martyr in the cause of truth (V, vii). He casts himself in the role
of such figures in order to speak to us: he speaks as Dante in
III, i, as the author of the Book of Revelations in VI, iv:
'Ecoutez. Je suis Jean'. The next step is not just to impersonate
them, but to remain himself and simultaneously see himself as
them. With his staff in 'Au fils d'un poëte' he becomes a
primitive traveller, a Wandering Jew eternally on the move: 'Sa
vie erre de grève en grève / Sous le souffle de Jéhovah' (V, ii,
19-20, p.239). In 'En frappant à une porte', the allusions to the
way of the Cross, the crown of thorns, and the wound, indicate
even more clearly an identification with Christ:

> J'ai sur tous mes travaux l'affront,
> Aux pieds la poudre, au cœur des plaies,
>   L'épine au front. (VI, xxiv, 22-24, p.385)

The list could be considerably extended. These parallels and
identifications suggest, not an irrepressible and absurd self-
aggrandizement, but rather one way that Hugo's life is given an
accessible and significant form. As well as adapting it to a
conventional and linear structure, he invests with authority the
persona, the voice with which he speaks, by assimilating familiar
myths. The key word here is perhaps assimilation. Hugo does
not simply adapt himself to the figures evoked, but adapts *them*.
In 'Le poëme éploré se lamente' (I, ix), the poet is Prometheus
who moulds man 'dans l'argile sacrée', the rebel whom Zeus
punished by chaining him, 'seul sur son noir sommet', to the
Caucasus and by setting an eagle to devour his liver ('sans
épuiser son flanc'). But Prometheus is also assimilated to Christ,
not only by the wound in his side, but also, in the final line, by
being nailed rather than chained, and to a skull: 'C'est ... / Sur
ton crâne géant qu'est cloué Prométhée'. Golgotha, the hill of
the Crucifixion, means 'the place of a skull'. By this assimilation
of both figures to the poet, the poem goes beyond its simple

explicit theme, namely that the poet has lived and suffered vicariously in his creatures, to suggest both the power of the poet as creator, and the suffering of the poet as heroic victim for all humanity.

2. The Itinerary of the Poet

> 'Dante tord toute l'ombre et toute la
> clarté dans une spirale monstrueuse. Cela
> descend, puis cela monte.' (*I*, XII, p.183)

In the Preface, Hugo underlines the main structural feature of
Les Contemplations: two halves, *Autrefois*, *Aujourd'hui*,
separated by 'le tombeau', the death of Léopoldine in 1843.
Although the starting-point, 1830, has several possible
resonances — it is the date of Hugo's first stage success,
Hernani, and, politically, of the July Revolution — it serves
above all as a memorable round number. Moreover, since the
year of publication[3] and of the last-dated poems (VI, xxi, xxiii)
is 1856, it gives an equal number of years to each half of the
volume.

The opening poem establishes the central themes: man and his
place in the universe, observed by a poet rooted in contingent
experience ('Un jour je vis, debout au bord des flots mouvants
...'), but at the same time open to the absolute, to 'l'autre
abîme' (p.31). It also introduces images that will run throughout
the volume, developing new associations as it progresses: the
stars, the sea, the wind. The star reappears to guide the poet,
notably in 'Magnitudo parvi' (III, xxx), and in IV, xvii, where
Léopoldine and Charles are transformed into 'deux étoiles'. The
sea, which evokes the unknown, the formless, is linked with exile
in Book V, with death in Book VI; the wind is often linked with
the idea of the creative power of God (e.g. VI, ix).

In the first book, 'Aurore', the young poet discovers nature,
recalls the first stirrings of love, and shows his love for children.
In his youthful enthusiasm he breaks with the artificial constraints of tradition, above all in literature (I, vii, xxvi). The title

---

[3] *Aujourd'hui* was dated in the first edition '1843-1855'; the second Paris edition
of May 1856 corrected the latter date to 1856.

of Book II, 'L'Ame en fleur', links man and nature; it brings a deeper understanding of the significance of love, a love set in nature and defying social conventions, continuing the theme of revolt. In Book III the maturing poet moves beyond his world of self-contained happiness and discovers the suffering, cruelty, ambitions, and follies that characterize the world of man. This evil is contrasted with the goodness and harmony of nature; it raises a question ('?', III, xi) to which the poet as yet has no answer, although various ideas appear that are later to fit into or be superseded by the revelations of Book VI. Book III ends, typically, with a key transitional poem: the poet, talking to his daughter, as in I, i and the Epilogue, observes a shepherd who, isolated from society, ignorant, humble, can attain an intuitive understanding of the mystery of the universe. This, and not revolt, nor political activity, seems to be the way ahead. But although Hugo outlines a programme for 'contemplation' and spiritual discovery, it is something the poet has only observed in another person whom he clearly distinguishes from himself and ordinary mortals.

Book IV is not concerned with the actual drowning of Léopoldine, but with the poet's reaction to this first irruption of the absurd into his own life. The dating and, above all, the order of the poems suggest a movement from initial despair, disbelief, and revolt against God, to acceptance and submission, interrupted by nostalgic memories. These feelings the poet shares with all men. IV, iii also introduces two themes which set him apart: the conflict between his public duty and the private grief that absorbs him, and the sense that the seer cannot have both human happiness and insight. The exile of Book V completes the making of the seer: it separates him from his previous life and friends, and is compared to a tomb (notably in V, i), a symbolic anticipation of the death which brings revelations. 'Mourir, c'est connaître' (III, xxx, 444, p.192). Themes from earlier books: nature, suffering, are taken up again with a changed emphasis that prepares Book VI. After alternating between exuberant confidence in the poet-seer and moments of humility, doubt, and even terror, book VI culminates in the revelation of 'Ce que dit la bouche d'ombre' (VI, xxvi). The volume closes with an

Epilogue addressed 'A celle qui est restée en France',
Léopoldine; in this flexibly organized reprise of the main themes
of the volume, the poet, both as father and seer, finally attains a
degree of serenity.

The itinerary that Hugo creates, from optimism through
doubt and suffering to renewed confidence, can be seen as
common to all men in the first four books: 'la vie d'un homme',
and 'la vie des autres hommes aussi' (Preface, p.28). But a preoccupation with the specific role of the poet develops throughout the volume. In the final two books, the poet not only reaches
'l'énigme du cercueil', as do all men, but also explores it. Here
the poet is privileged not only in the way that he can express his
experiences, but also in the nature of these experiences. The
structure of the volume can add to the meaning of individual
poems by the way they are situated in this dual itinerary. The
poem on 'Le Mendiant' (V, ix) assumes added significance for
being set in the section where the poet is in exile; its theme, that
of the spiritual awareness of the social outcast, is reinforced by
its echo of III, xxx and its anticipation of the poem on prayer,
VI, i. But though Hugo himself stressed the rigour of the
structure,[4] we should be wary of explaining every detail in terms
of the overall movement. Hugo often ends a poem with a
powerful but ambiguous image, such as the heather and holly of
IV, xiv, or the sea-holly of V, xiii. To subordinate these to the
structure, for instance by seeing these flowers echoed in 'J'ai
cueilli cette fleur' (V, xxiv), is to risk that danger of schematism
which led an early critic to read the encounter with the girl in
I, xxi as the union of the poet and democracy. The unit of
meaning and artistic value remains the poem, embodying an
individual facet of experience; it may gain by its context, but it
has to work as a poem in its own right.

---

[4] 'Les pièces de ce diable de recueil sont comme les pierres d'une voûte.
Impossible de les déplacer' (*I*, IX, p.1094). Yet he added a new poem at the last
moment to avoid repeating rhymes in successive poems: *26*, p.76 (II, viii).

3. *The Eye of the Poet*

'Lucrèce tourne le dos à l'humanité et regarde fixement l'énigme.' (*I*, XII, p.178)

It is a commonplace to stress the importance of the visual to Hugo; he himself confessed: 'Je suis un grand regardeur de toutes choses' (*1*, VI, p.466).[5] He uses the noun *contemplation* and the verb *contempler* frequently in the volume,[6] to suggest a range of activities, predominantly, but not solely, visual; sometimes in a broad sense, sometimes with a more restricted and personal, quasi-technical value, to designate an activity specific to man, who is a combination of reason and intuition. Hugo's formulation clearly implies the primacy of intuition: 'l'homme qui contemple, / ... Etre en qui l'instinct vit dans la raison dissous' (VI, xxvi, 231-33, p.393).

From the opening line of the first poem, the emphasis is on what the poet sees: 'Un jour, je vis ...' This is a pattern which recurs several times: see, for instance, the first lines of III, i ('Un soir, dans le chemin je vis ...'), V, xviii, and VI, i. Several poems capture an experience that is intensely visual. In 'Mes deux filles' (I, iii), the poet explicitly enjoins us to observe: 'Voyez'. He records, in the present tense, a moment of multiple visual impressions: the falling evening, the carnations in the breeze with their fragile stalks — the central rhyme suggestively coupling 'elles' with 'frêles' — together with visual images: the girls are *seen as* white birds, the flowers are seen as butterflies. All these impressions combine in their associations of beauty,

---

[5] He was a talented and individual draughtsman — an activity about which he was uncharacteristically modest: 'Cela m'amuse entre deux strophes' (to Baudelaire, *1*, XI, p.1098).

[6] For a fuller exploration of the words, see Moreau, *28*, pp.3-9, and Gaudon, *12*, pp.25-41.

innocence, and delicacy, to suggest, not only the qualities of the girls, but also those of the moment itself, fleeting and magically immobilized. The final image sums up this sense both of arrested movement and of attentiveness: the flowers seem 'un vol de papillons arrêté dans l'extase'.

But there are few poems that are purely visual. Other senses are constantly involved in the 'spectacle' of nature: not only colours are evoked in 'Premier mai' (II, i), but also scents and sounds. Moreover, the visual is constantly accompanied by an emotional response to the scene, and by a quest for, or a sense of, its meaning. It is revealing that *voir* in Hugo usually implies, not just seeing, but grasping or understanding a truth. Seeing is knowing: 'Tu verras' is the same as 'Tu le sauras' (VI, xxvi, 197-98, p.392); and this strongly positive sense comes over in the swift's dictum: 'Et voir la vérité, c'est trouver la vertu' (III, viii, 36). It is worth examining how in 'A Villequier' (IV, xv), a poem concerned with feelings and ideas, Hugo constantly uses expressions concerned with sight, more or less metaphorically, to convey the way he is aware of things ('voyant ma petitesse'), has things present to his mind ('je verrai cet instant ...'), experiences things ('quand on a vu ...'), as if it were the main way by which we can know, experience, even possess things: 'Tout ce qu'il voit est court, inutile et fuyant'. Visual perception leads to understanding; conversely, understanding is presented as a visual experience.

The poet's quest for meaning is implicit in the recurring image of the poet 'reading' the book of nature, albeit fleetingly:

> Les plaines où le ciel aide l'herbe à germer,
> L'eau, les prés, sont autant de phrases où le sage
> Voit serpenter des sens qu'il saisit au passage. (III, viii)

The owl nailed to the door (III, xiii), the beggar (V, ix) yield their message; the lowing of the cattle (V, xvii) becomes meaningful *voix* whose exhortations the poet translates into human language. Here Hugo is taking a single object and seeing the meaning that lies behind it; elsewhere he takes a diversity of objects and suggests the unity that links them. In 'Unité' a series of contrasts between the sun and the flower (great/small, eternal/transitory, noble/familiar) culminates in the daisy's assertion of similarity: 'Et moi, j'ai des rayons aussi!' (I, xxv). The sense of this reply is not immediately clear: aesthetic vindication of the apparently ill-favoured? sense of the divine (*rayons*) in everything? We are forced to *see* the similarity and reflect on its implications. Elsewhere Hugo is more explicit: an exuberant life runs through the diverse aspects of nature in 'Le firmament est plein de la vaste clarté', progressing through the poem from carefree fun to solemn celebration: 'Tout regorge de sève et de vie et de bruit' (I, iv). The sense of a unifying life-force permeating nature is powerfully suggested in 'Mugitusque boum' (V, xvii) and 'Eclaircie' (VI, x), and points towards God as the unity and permanence behind the multiple and changing facets of creation. This is sometimes explicit, notably in section vii of 'Les Mages' (VI, xxiii); arguably it is less effective then:

> L'éternel est écrit dans ce qui dure peu;
> Toute l'immensité, sombre, bleue, étoilée,
> Traverse l'humble fleur, du penseur contemplée;
> On voit les champs, mais c'est de Dieu qu'on s'eblouit.
>
> (III, viii)

When contemplating nature at night, the poet's meditation is presented sometimes as a looking inwards with the help of an 'œil intérieur', as in 'Saturne' (III, iii), sometimes as a looking beyond things, as in 'Magnitudo parvi', Hugo's most detailed exposition of the activity of contemplation. The visionary *pâtre* of the poem 'regarde tant la nature, / Que la nature a disparu', and Hugo affirms, paradoxically: 'contempler les choses, / C'est finir par ne plus les voir' (III, xxx, 566-67, p.196). There follows a lengthy enumeration of the aspects of nature that the *pâtre* no longer sees: 'Il ne voit plus le ver qui rampe, / La feuille morte ...', culminating in the stars, and the affirmation of what he *does* see: 'Il voit Dieu!' But this is the experience of the *pâtre*, not of Hugo. The ultimate cannot really be visualized or described. Some poems may *approach* it, for instance 'Ibo' (VI, ii), a poem notable for its confident use of the future tense, from the title ('I shall go') onwards; but by the end of the poem, we are still only nearing the threshold.

The visionary quest remains intensely visual in Hugo. 'Mors', with its sense of observed reality, renews the traditional allegorical representation of Death:

> Je vis cette faucheuse. Elle était dans son champ.
> Elle allait à grands pas moissonnant et fauchant,
> Noir squelette laissant passer le crépuscule. (IV, xvi)

The visualization of the scene is very Hugolian in its use of contrast and bold gestures, its dynamism, and its use of impressions with immediately intelligible connotations: 'noir' = sinister; dusk = age. In other poems the response to the unknown is equally visual but less conventional, as in the paradoxical description at the start of 'Le Pont' of something dark, contourless, and motionless:

> J'avais devant les yeux les ténèbres. L'abîme
> Qui n'a pas de rivage et qui n'a pas de cime
> Etait là, morne, immense; et rien n'y remuait. (VI, i)

Again the scene has an emotional charge: 'morne'. The moods aroused by the spectacles contemplated show a Hugolian polarization. Initially, comprehension of the harmony of nature leads to exaltation, and a sense of acceptance by nature, of participation in its life:

> La contemplation m'emplit le cœur d'amour. (III, xxiv)

Although this feeling is still found later ('Eclaircie', VI, x), as the volume progresses the poet is increasingly a solitary, disturbing figure ('Pasteurs et troupeaux', V, xxiii), and the mood of his meditation slides into awe, even fear. In the visionary poems of book VI, terror is evoked by the familiar world transformed, as at the start of 'A la fenêtre, pendant la nuit' (VI, ix), and by the unknown:

Nous regardons trembler l'ombre indéterminée.
Nous sommes accoudés sur notre destinée,
    L'œil fixe et l'esprit frémissant. (VI, xiv)

Here we see two of the recurrent causes of fear, coupled paradoxically with an attentive eagerness: the formless, and the
vertigo induced by leaning as if over a bottomless pit or well.
Both recur in the final poem of the volume:

Deviens le grand œil fixe ouvert sur le grand tout.
Penche-toi sur l'énigme où l'être se dissout.
                                ('A celle ...', lines 243-44, p.418)

This polarization of moods that accompanies the idea of
seeing is found with the reciprocal theme of being seen. The
watching eye can offer guidance, protection, stability, re-
assurance. It can be human, and female:

Tu me regardais, dans ma nuit,
Avec ton beau regard d'étoile,
    Qui m'éblouit. (II, x)

It can be the traditional, and also Biblical, eye of God (see e.g.
Ezekiel 7. 4), as at the end of 'Eclaircie': 'Tout est doux, calme,
heureux, apaisé: Dieu regarde' (VI, x). But critical or hostile
eyes are more frequent, like the 'yeux obliques et méchants' (II,
xvi) of society from which the lovers hide. In the course of the
volume, we find significantly varied responses to the gazes of the
poet's dog (V, xi), the lion (III, xix), the moon (V, xiii), and
Egyptian statues (I, vi). If accompanied by a sense of sin, the
idea of being seen will intensify guilt, as in 'Aux anges qui nous
voient': 'Oh! cachez-moi, profondes nuits!' (VI, xii). Hugo can
turn the whole physical world into a surveillance system:

L'espace sait, regarde, écoute. Il est rempli
D'oreilles sous la tombe, et d'yeux dans les ténèbres.
                                                          (VI, iii)

This appeal to basic human fears underlies the terror of the wicked man, who, in 'Joies du soir', *sees* at the moment of his death 'la face vague et sombre et l'œil fixe de Dieu' (III, xxvi). The fixity of the eye here suggests relentless scrutiny, rather than reassuring stability.

The visual is fundamental to Hugo; but a strong case could be made for the centrality of the aural and the oral in *Les Contemplations*. Some poems are totally (VI, xii) or mainly (VI, xx) in dialogue form. 'Ibo' starts with the urgent question: 'Dites, pourquoi' (VI, ii); and voices speak and reveal things to the poet from the 'voix dont mes yeux / Ne voyaient pas la bouche' of the opening poem, via 'ce que le vent m'a dit sur la montagne' (III, xii), to the 'bouche d'ombre' (VI, xxvi). The universe is not only a book to be read visually, it is also voices to be listened to. 'Tout dit dans l'infini quelque chose à quelqu'un'; 'tout parle' (VI, xxvi, 42, 46, p.387): flowers, trees (I, ii), birds (I, xviii; III, ix), cattle (V, xvii), the owl (III, xiii).[7] The poet *talks* to us both as himself: 'Ecoutez', he says at the start of 'Melancholia' (III, ii), and through other figures: 'Ecoutez. Je suis Jean' (VI, iv). He talks to his daughter (IV, xiv, and the final poem), to a ghost (VI, xv), and to God, notably in 'A Villequier' (IV, xv). If 'Un jour, je vis ...' is characteristically Hugolian in its dramatic immediacy, so is: 'Une nuit, un esprit me parla dans un rêve, / Et me dit ...' (VI, xviii). Hugo can startle us by turning things into eyes, notably the globe which 'devient un œil énorme et regarde la nuit' (I, iv); but he also does so with the self-transformation of 'Ibo': 'Je suis ... la bouche / Du clairon noir' (VI, ii, 101-04, p.301). This image brings us back to the visual: we see the bugle as much as hear it; and the following chapters will frequently indicate that a further reason for privileging the visual in Hugo is its role in his imagery, which is, in a very real sense, the way that he *sees* things.

[7] See below, p.66, on prosopopoeia.

4. Poetry and Politics

'Barbare, extravagant, emphatique, anti-
thétique, boursouflé, absurde, telle est la
sentence rendue contre lui par la
rhétorique officielle d'à présent.' (*I*, XII,
p.204; Æschylus)

'Ajoutons ceci, être hiératique, cela ne
l'empêchait pas d'être démotique. Eschyle
aimait le peuple, et le peuple l'adorait.'
(*I*, XII, p.218)

If I link these two preoccupations, it is because Hugo himself
constantly does so. The first, and most memorable, occasion is
in 'Réponse à un acte d'accusation' (I, vii), which purports to be
a reply to an accusation that he has defied taste and literary
convention, an accusation which he joyfully endorses. He
presents pre-Romantic verse as shackled by the rigid formal constraints of the classical alexandrine, by a limited 'poetic'
vocabulary of noble words that excluded the precise and the
realistic, and by rhetorical figures. This state of affairs is set in
parallel with the pre-revolutionary *ancien régime* with its
separate castes, its rigid hierarchy and etiquette: 'l'idiome ...
était l'image du royaume'. His poetic counterpart to the French
Revolution has overthrown the hierarchy of noble words in
literature: '[Je] déclarai les mots égaux, libres, majeurs' (I, vii,
75, p.44).

The argument, if taken literally, may seem dubious. Does a
hierarchy of vocabulary constitute injustice? Do words have
'verbal rights'? Although Hugo says that he will limit his
argument to the question of form, the essential justification for
his revolution lies in the link between form and content. This is
implicit in 'A André Chénier' (I, v), an injunction by nature, in
the person of a bullfinch, telling the poet to change his form in

order to capture the diversity shown by nature. For Hugo, the traditional noble language inhibited expression of some reality; his formal innovations, namely a wider and more specific vocabulary and a freer alexandrine, are needed to explore new areas of 'le vrai' and 'l'imagination' (I, vii, 194-95, p.47). These are what Hugo will explore in the immensely varied poems of *Les Contemplations*: nature, man, and society (now that the Muse can again 'pleurer sur la misère humaine', line 206, p.47), and the imagination's insight into the universe.

What is central for Hugo is expressing 'le vrai' and 'l'imagination'; it follows that he will use the appropriate linguistic means. One can find him using ones that he would seem to exclude in the 'Réponse': the noble alternatives *astre* (for *étoile*), *nocher* (for *marin*, in V, iv). He claims:

> Je nommai le cochon par son nom; pourquoi pas?
> Guichardin [a Florentine historian] a nommé le Borgia!
>
> (I, vii, 80-81, p.44)

But he writes 'le porc Borgia' (VI, xxvi, 674, p.406). He claims: 'J'ai de la périphrase écrasé les spirales' (I, vii, 150, p.46), but the rhetorical figures that he uses include not only periphrasis, but also, as we shall see, chiasmus, prosopopoeia, hypallage.[8] The 'Réponse' is not so much *against* traditional poetic language, as *for* a diversity that would include the classical poetic language as much as the realistic, when appropriate. The *porc* just quoted is 'right', and consequently expressive, alive, because of its sound: [pɔʀ bɔʀʒia]. The very formalised diction of the start of the final poem (p.411) fits the solemn, ritualistic moment that it evokes. In Hugo, both traditional literary devices and formal innovations are means of embodying his vision of the world, of making us also '[ouvrir] les yeux sur la nature' (I, vii, 32, p.43).

For Hugo, language can not only express reality, it can change it. In the final section of the 'Réponse', political and literary

---

[8] Chiasmus: inversion in a second phrase of the word order of the first (see below, p.62); for prosopopoeia, the use of a pretended speaker, see p.66; for hypallage, the transference of an adjective to a word in the sentence to which it does not strictly apply, see p.77.

revolutions are not just set in parallel, but linked, to suggest that prose, verse, drama play a key role in dissipating prejudice and implementing progress in society. The theme of the power of language is exuberantly developed in the following poem, 'Suite' (I, viii). After an initial assertion that words are beings with a life of their own, we are confronted with a proliferation of ideas. Some of these are fanciful: the word has a mind of its own, 'veut, ne veut pas'; some are primitive and magical: language not only illuminates the world, like light, but antedates it, since it was the word of God that created the world; others are thought-provoking: through language, man knows and masters the world, and 'le mot tient sous ses pieds le globe et l'asservit' (line 41, p.49). But whether Hugo's ideas are eccentric, primitive or trite (e.g. the power of slogans), what underlies them all is a conviction of the power of language over the world and over feelings, and by implication of the special role of the poet who uses language. From 'ce troupeau de signes et de sons ... / Naissent les cris, les chants, les soupirs, les harangues' (I, viii, 37-39, p.49).

The most immediately intelligible aspect of this view of language is the idea that a liberated language serves human freedom, and is a weapon against tyranny, oppression, and obscurantism: 'la main courroucée / Qui délivre le mot, délivre la pensée' (I, vii, 153-54, p.46). The cruelties and injustices it has to combat emerge in Book III. Some poems evoke specific evils: war in 'La Source' (III, vi), poverty in 'Chose vue un jour de printemps' (III, xvii), capital punishment in 'La Nature' (III, xxix). The long poem 'Melancholia' (III, ii) presents a series of instances, drawn from the world of man, of cruelty and unmerited suffering. We see, notably, the hungry working mother whose husband drinks; the orphan forced into prostitution by poverty; the poor man sentenced to hard labour for stealing a loaf to feed his family, as in *Les Misérables*; the genius scorned in his lifetime, hypocritically praised by posterity; the carthorse beaten to death by a drunken master; the veteran of the Napoleonic wars reduced to penury... In most cases the victim, innocent and helpless through age, sex or status, is set against a person or group that is indifferent, heartlessly mocking, or corruptly triumphant. The appeal to our pity is clear; but should our indignation be directed at society as it is constituted, or at individuals, who range from the uncomprehending to the corrupt and the brutal? Both this poem, and '?' (III, xi), which encompasses an even wider range of violence by man, animals, and the elements, limit themselves to presenting the fact of unjust human suffering, and contrasting it with the refuge offered by nature (in the final line of 'Melancholia') or with the radiant beauty of the earth seen as a star in the sky (in '?'). The very title '?' neatly indicates that the poet can neither see why such suffering exists, nor suggest what sort of measures might relieve it. The final section of 'Melancholia', which contrasts the poor and the rich in the towns, ends with a vision which is vivid, dramatic, but ambiguous. The guillotine appears above the rich who dance and gamble:

> Deux poteaux soutenant un triangle hideux,
> Qui sortent lentement du noir pavé des villes...
>
> (III, ii, 334-35, p.135)

Does this suggest a resurgence of revolutionary violence, or is Hugo saying that it is the rich who use the guillotine as an instrument of oppression?[9] The poem presents a vivid image of injustice and its potential for violence, but nothing that could be construed as social analysis or political solution.

At the end of Book V, another major poem, 'Les Malheureux', returns to the question of the suffering of the innocent, but from a metaphysical rather than a social point of view, and with a shift of emphasis as regards the victims. The suffering victims of 'Melancholia', apart from the *homme de génie*, are not only crushed by their plight and unable to struggle, but also unaware, lacking the inner strength that might come from conviction of a goal. The children 'ne comprennent rien à leur destin, hélas!' (III, ii, 126, p.129); the horse is overwhelmed by his task and the brutality of his master:

[9] III, xxix condemns capital punishment, but V, iii, 231, p.247, seems to justify the 'mal passager' of revolutionary violence by the 'bien éternel' that it allows.

> Il sent l'ombre sur lui peser; il ne sait pas,
> Sous le bloc qui l'écrase et le fouet qui l'assomme,
> Ce que lui veut la pierre et ce que lui veut l'homme.
>
> (lines 158-60, p.130)

The victims of 'Les Malheureux' are in contrast sustained by their knowledge that they are in the right. Starting with the *pauvre* and progressing through a series of others most of whom died for their beliefs, they can all say: 'Je suis heureux' (line 56, p.286). They knew they were right; like the *pauvre*, they can say: 'Je n'ai point fait de mal'; for them, humiliation and physical suffering are nothing alongside spiritual certainty and the immortal soul. The noblest thing for man,

> C'est chute, abaissement, misère extérieure,
> Acceptés pour garder la grandeur du dedans.
>
> (lines 238-39, p.291)

Hugo now presents *all* who suffer, 'tous les souffrants' (line 261, p.292) as happy, 'la plaie au sein, la joie au cœur', deserving admiration rather than pity. Pity, and not indignation, should be reserved for the cruel and wicked; it is they who are the true *malheureux*; as they say, 'Nous sommes ceux qui font le mal; et, comme / C'est nous qui le faisons, c'est nous qui le souffrons' (lines 314-15, p.294). They suffer because they are cut off from God and what He represents: harmony and love. They consequently aspire to be reconciled with God, and Hugo will later present an explanation of how this can be achieved in 'Ce que dit la bouche d'ombre' (VI, xxvi).

If Book III presented suffering in terms of instances of social injustice, this followed on from the idea of poetry as an instrument of progress: the poet operated a revolution in his own domain, language, and illuminated areas of society susceptible to action and reform, but without suggesting solutions. Hugo's preoccupation in later books is still very much with suffering, but in Books IV and V it is with his *personal* suffering as father and exile; in Book VI, it is with those who inflict it and their punishment. The only answer suggested to the question as to *why* apparently innocent humans suffer[10] would seem to be that this is a necessary part of an imperfect world, and essential to the maintenance of the doubt without which human freewill and choice would have no value.

What sort of poems does Hugo write on these themes? Instead of the abstract arguments that one might expect, we find ones sustained by vivid images; and the voice that we hear is not dispassionate, but intensely personal and charged with emotion. The 'Réponse à un acte d'accusation' gives both a caricatural version of the accusations made against Hugo: 'Donc, c'est moi qui suis l'ogre ...', and a self-justification that is provocatively exaggerated. It develops by taking an idea and elaborating on it in an infinitely extensible accumulation of examples and metaphors. (The sequence of alexandrines in *rimes plates*: *aabbcc ...*, could likewise continue indefinitely.) The overall parallels classicism/*ancien régime*, literary revolution/French Revolution provide a framework for individual variations which are comic in their precision, and leap from one incongruity to the next. The Classical Muses sing a revolutionary song:

> Les neuf muses, seins nus, chantaient la Carmagnole;
> L'emphase frissonna dans sa fraise espagnole;
>
> > (I, vii, 89-90, p.44)

and the contrast restraint/liberty moves to the level of dress; the alliterations underline the shudder of horror of the *classique*. Ingenious and precise images illustrate not only the general spirit, but also details of Hugo's innovations. This is how he defends his abandonment of the regular central caesura dividing the twelve-syllable alexandrine into two equal halves with a stress on the sixth syllable:

> Le vers, qui sur son front
> Jadis portait toujours douze plumes en rond,
> Et sans cesse sautait sur la double raquette
> Qu'on nomme prosodie et qu'on nomme étiquette,

---

[10] Suffering *outside* the human world is part of the process of retribution outlined in VI, xxvi.

Rompt désormais la règle et trompe le ciseau,
Et s'échappe, volant qui se change en oiseau,
De la cage césure, et fuit vers la ravine,
Et vole dans le cieux, alouette divine. (lines 183-90, p.47)

Hugo sees the classical alexandrine as a shuttlecock (*volant*) whose regular to-and-fro represents the two symmetrical halves of the line, and his freer line as a bird. He simultaneously continues previous images in the contrast court etiquette/nature, the ravine, introduces new ones with the ruthlessly truncating *ciseau*, and prepares the lyrical movement of the end of the poem with the shift from 'dans les cieux' to 'divine'.

Comic verve is one of Hugo's main weapons. He parodies Genesis: 'J'ai dit à l'ombre: "Sois!"' (line 4, p.42); the Marseillaise, which was a revolutionary hymn at this time: 'Aux armes, prose et vers! formez vos bataillons!' (line 115, p.45); the revolutionary slogan 'Guerre aux châteaux, paix aux chaumières' in: 'Guerre à la rhétorique et paix à la syntaxe!' (line 121, p.45). He indulges in pure verbal fun: in 'On vit trembler l'athos, l'ithos et le pathos' (line 123, p.45), the last two are literary terms, but the first exists only as a proper noun: a Greek mountain — and one of Dumas's musketeers. Even rhyme is not a difficulty, but rather a source of fun and an occasion for ingenuity: 'ABCD' rhymes with 'débordé' (lines 27-28, p.42). It is in such poems that Hugo's rhymes are often richest, with proper names in particular provoking ingenious ideas. The rhymes 'génisse'/'Bérénice' (lines 85-86, p.44) and 'jusqu'à la lie'/'Athalie' (lines 129-30, p.45) provide incongruous companions for Racine's heroines.

This technique of arguing through an accumulation of loosely related images works by creating a disparate and dense metaphorical texture, which is itself a defiance of the Classical ideals of restraint and coherence. But this density is the result in part of the use of traditional rhetorical figures. Continuing his argument in 'Quelques mots à un autre', Hugo says to the defenders of tradition:

Le drame échevelé fait peur à vos fronts chauves.

(I, xxvi, 82, p.81)

Metonymy is the figure by which one word replaces another with which it stands in a constant relationship: e.g. 'crown' for 'king'. It is by metonymy that 'fronts' stands for the minds, the intellectual and aesthetic response, of the *classiques*; at the same time the sense is extended from 'forehead' (eyebrows to hairline) to the whole head, so that it can be qualified with 'chauve', implying that the critics are old and behind the times. In contrast 'échevelé' has not only its usual sense when coupled with 'drame': 'wild', 'frenzied', but also that of 'dishevelled', evoking metonymically wild-haired youth. The line thus suggests a series of oppositions to discredit the opponents of Romantic drama: youth/age, violence/restraint, passion/intellect, boldness/timidity.

If, for Hugo, restraint is one obstacle to be overthrown in order to capture reality, taste is another. 'Sans pudeur, on écrit comme on pense' (I, xxvi, 98, p.81); and an exuberant series of images evokes an impudently immodest nature flaunting its sexuality (I, xxvi, 106-29, p.82). We cannot carp at the resultant poem for being overlong, outrageous, and lacking a sense of propriety without putting ourselves into the category that Hugo is mocking. At the same time it does seem appropriate to criticize him when the verve and inventiveness of the monologue flag, as they do in parts of 'A propos d'Horace' (I, xiii).

There is a second sense in which these poems could be said to rely for their impact on the image. In 'Melancholia' we are struck by a sequence of individual instances of injustice, presented abruptly, without transition, in a sequence of *rimes plates*:

> Une femme au profil décharné,
> Maigre, blême, portant un enfant étonné,
> *Est là* qui se lamente au milieu de la rue.

(III, ii, 1-3; my italics)

Adapting the title of 'Chose vue un jour de printemps' (III, xvii), one could term these *choses vues*.[11] Not that they were actually seen by Hugo: that of III, xvii is in fact based on a prose item from a newspaper of 1852, which was in turn (though Hugo probably did not know this) based on a prizewinning but prosaic poem of 1851, 'Les Enfants de la morte', by Charles Lafont. It is Hugo's technique that creates the impression of immediacy: the use of the present tense; the paucity of metaphor or simile, creating the effect of the factual; the poet's insistence that he is directly presenting the scene, rather than commenting on it: 'Ecoutez', 'Regardez' (III, ii, 1, 52, pp.126, 127).

In these poems it is often difficult not to react against what now seems excessive sentimentality. The episode of the death of the horse in 'Melancholia', 'Le Revenant' (III, xxiii), 'Le Maître d'études' (III, xvi) were among the most immediately popular poems of the volume at the time of its publication. In them we find helpless and innocent victims, and an intensification of both their plight and their virtue in such a way as to provoke instant emotional response, untroubled by the complexity of reality, the possibility of other points of view. The horse's driver is a drunken brute; the poor, noble and persecuted schoolmaster sacrifices himself not only for his pupils, but also, perhaps, for his parents 'qu'il soutient en secret' (III, xvi, 74, p.156); he suffers, but is not embittered. 'Chose vue ...' (III, xvii) attacks our sympathy with four weeping orphans, the oldest aged 6, and the virtues of their mother and father, to awaken our sense of social injustice in a very *general* sense: 'Oh! la faim, c'est le crime public'. We might now reflect that the *social* injustice does not depend on their virtue.

A more positive quality in these *choses vues* is Hugo's dramatic sense. In 'Le Mendiant' (V, ix) he moves skilfully from an opening narrative which introduces the beggar and the bad weather in the first line, to a first statement of what the beggar does: pray, closing with the word 'Dieu' (line 9). The poet's gesture of hospitality then leads to a dialogue whose very banality suggests that something more important is at stake, and

---

[11] The title was given to posthumous collections of notes and anecdotes from Hugo's papers.

then to the description of the beggar's coat hanging in front of the fire. Twice the alexandrine shifts from informality to dignity, and the syntax from simplicity to complexity; the beggar's prosaic 'manteau' becomes a 'bure': homespun, but also often used of a monk's frock. The factual description and the small-scale domestic scene give way to the transformation, in the eye of the poet, of the ragged coat into the night sky filled with stars, as he sees the fire, intensified into a *fournaise*, shining through its holes (Hugo imagines the stars as holes through which shines a radiance from beyond: see I, x). This final image suggests the meaning of the scene: the spiritual greatness that can lie in someone living in isolation and humility, but 'plein de prières'. There is no need for Hugo to develop it explicitly.

The success of 'Le Mendiant' can be gauged by comparing it with a similar but less effective poem-anecdote, 'Je payai le pêcheur' (V, xxii), where the poet purchases a crab, 'bête horrible', from a fisherman, is nearly bitten, and throws it back into the sea. It lacks progression in tone, it is full from the start of emphatic adjectives, its end is pat and sententious: 'l'homme rend le bien au monstre pour le mal', and it strikes a note of incongruous comedy when we see the poet struggling with the crab (Hugo forgets that it is not the teeth of crabs that present a danger): 'ses dents cherchaient mes doigts'. 'Le Mendiant', in constrast, develops an economical narrative that both seems realistic and everyday, and also has a traditional mythical resonance, recalling the stories of Christ appearing in the guise of a beggar, or a leper, and revealing himself when helped. 'Les Malheureux', though suffering from some overlong passages of argument and illustration, is another poem that strikes the imagination at the end, combining the visual and the mythic in its vivid picture of Adam and Eve, alone in face of an increasingly vast landscape, as evening and silence gradually give way to night and their tears over the first innocent victim and the first murderer. This shift of scale and tone at the end of the poem, the movement from reality to imagination or myth, is characteristic of Hugo, and is shared both by the poem (e.g. the 'Réponse') that persuades or overwhelms with a breakneck succession of surprising images, and by the poem that moves or conveys an idea through the use of an anecdote or *chose vue*. I shall return to it in the next chapter.

5. Love

'Çà et là une vaste image de l'accouple-
ment s'ébauche dans la forêt, *Tunc Venus
in sylvis jungebat corpora amantum*; et la
forêt, c'est la nature.' (*I*, XII, pp.177-78;
Lucretius)

The first poems in *Les Contemplations* to evoke love are nostalgic recollections of youth, its innocence, its adventures, and sometimes its missed opportunities, as in 'Vieille chanson du jeune temps' (I, xix). The title suggests an attitude or ironic amusement towards the age-old naivety of youth: the poem recalls the lack of enterprise of an adolescent who fails to see the encouragement of an older girl. But the elements of humour ('Les rossignols chantaient Rose / Et les merles me sifflaient') are combined with an emotional charge created by the simple and direct language, by the way the girl is shown in instinctive harmony with a wild nature, picking a blackberry, bathing her bare foot in a stream, entering the woods, and by the humanizing and eroticizing of nature, which seems to encourage the young pair:

Et la nature amoureuse
Dormait dans les grands bois sourds. (I, xix, 23-24, p.72)

Hugo returns to the same motifs: fruit, birds singing, feet in stream, woods, in other poems, but with a change of tone. 'Elle était déchaussée' (I, xxi) and 'Nous allions au verger ...' (II, vii) are poems of spontaneous male desire in a natural setting. If it is true, as Jean Prévost has argued, that the poem of straight-forward desire is of limited interest, since 'le désir fait courir le poète vers sa belle, et l'empêche de raffiner sur ses sentiments',[12]

---

[12] *Baudelaire*, Paris: Mercure de France, 1964, p.203.

the poems nevertheless achieve a wider resonance through their use of setting and their sense of the moment, of time. In both the physicality of the girl is stressed: in II, vii her arms, breasts, fingers, leg, teeth, and mouth are all glimpsed; in I, xxi the girl, 'déchaussée', 'décoiffée', the opposite of civilized, by the stream, amidst the rushes, is literally immersed in nature. In this poem, the poet initially invites her; but then it is she who moves towards him, as if taking the initiative, as nature is suffused with exaltation and sexuality in the exclamations of lines 12-13:

> Oh! comme les oiseaux chantaient au fond des bois!
> Comme l'eau caressait doucement le rivage!

The poem ends, not with resolution of the situation, but with an expectant moment: the image of the girl *about* to join him. II, vii moves a stage further, but again the sense of the moment is crucial. Hugo underlines the mobility of all the elements of the picture evoked by memory (it is set in the imperfect): of the foliage ('les feuilles frissonnaient au vent'), of the light, of the girl in the tree. All combine to suggest the fleeting nature of the moment and of the just-captured kiss.

The link established between love and nature, and the contrast nature/society, are constants of Book II. The countryside often becomes a refuge for a love that is outside or in conflict with society (II, xvi, II, xxiii, 15-16); the happiness of love is seen as something that will provoke envy and hostility ('Eglogue', II, xii). This theme could be interpreted biographically: society disapproved of Hugo's adulterous affairs, and he escaped into the countryside around Paris with Juliette Drouet. But its function within the volume is to mark a first stage in alienation from society, an alienation that will culminate in exile (Book V) and which is a precondition for real insight. And love, too, contributes to the growth of this insight.

One thing that Hugo does not do, in the poems of Book II, is evoke particular women, or his reaction to them, in the way that Baudelaire, in a poem like 'La Chevelure', evokes what it is he sees in a certain woman. Nor does Hugo tell us much about himself as an individual by showing himself in love. What he

suggests is the effect of love: how it changes his awareness of the
world, of society, and especially of nature. To blame Hugo, as
does Fernand Gregh, for his inability to abandon himself to his
feelings ('Il manque de simplicité dans la tendresse, et, par con-
séquent, ses vers manquent de sincérité', *15*, p.277) is perhaps to
miss the point that the real interest of the emotion, for the poet,
is not in the emotion itself, but in this transformation that it
brings about. It also implies a questionable link between
simplicity and sincerity, to which I shall return in the next
chapter.

This role of love is hinted at even in a simple and apparently
conventional poem like 'Mon bras pressait ta taille frêle'. The
poet initially evokes a moment of physical intimacy and
describes the woman with images drawn from nature:

> Mon bras pressait ta taille frêle
> Et souple comme le roseau;
> Ton sein palpitait comme l'aile
>   D'un jeune oiseau. (II, x)

Then there is a transition, in a stanza dominated by the idea of
transformation: night falls outside, and love effects a change
'dans nos âmes'. The final stanza surprisingly reverses the initial
positions of male strength/female weakness, and the images for
the woman are now not natural, but celestial in both senses
('comme un ange', 'ton beau regard d'étoile'), dazzling the poet
'dans ma nuit': his state of suffering, or ignorance. The idea of
woman as a mediating power — the sole one between man and
the world — is spelt out rather more baldly in 'Je respire où tu
palpites':

> L'amour fait comprendre à l'âme
> L'univers, sombre et béni;
> Et cette petite flamme
> Seule éclaire l'infini. (II, xxv, 29-32, p.118)

This increased awareness consists above all of a deepened
response to the natural world. The love poems set in nature

bring out most clearly certain recurrent features which are characteristic of Hugo's presentation of natural phenomena generally. Love can heighten the sense of the unity of nature: it makes the poet aware both of the diversity of the manifestations of life and of their underlying single source:

> O champs! il savourait ces fleurs et cette femme.
> O bois! ô prés! nature où tout s'absorbe en en.
>
> (II, xvii)

This 'life' present in all nature could at times equally well be termed 'love'. When he is in love, man is part of this unity too; hence a reason for Hugo being able to affirm: 'notre amour, c'est Dieu' ('Billet du matin', II, xiv): if the life coursing through nature is God, when man is in love, he participates in this. Hugo draws constant parallels between man and nature 'in love', showing a reciprocal exchange of feelings:

> Et nous donnons notre fièvre
> Aux fleurs où nous appuyons
> Nos bouches, et notre lèvre
> Sent le baiser des rayons. (II, xxiii, 57-60, p.116)

The season is often spring, as in 'Premier mai' (II, i), accompanied by a sense of renewal, of rebirth, both of the individual in love and of nature as a whole. Nature is suddenly revealed as if just created for the first time, or created anew. In 'Après l'hiver', 'Tout revit, ma bien-aimée!' (II, xxiii). This at first sight merely conventional view is reinforced by insistent images: 'L'aurore où nous nous aimâmes / Semble renaître à nos yeux' (lines 21-22, p.114); 'Comme l'aube, tu me charmes' (line 37, p.115), and by the significant evocation of the first couple, and by implication of Edenic innocence:

> La nature, sœur jumelle
> D'Eve et d'Adam et du jour,
> Nous aime, nous berce ... (lines 41-43, p.115)

This innocence goes hand in hand with a strong element of sensuality, even sexuality, running through nature: 'nos caresses, / Toute l'ombre nous les rend' (lines 47-48, p.115), a sensuality which is perhaps most clearly marked in 'Crépuscule'. This in contrast is a poem of the evening, and the date 'août' is reinforced by the presence of cut corn and ripe fruit, though Hugo has rather unseasonably chosen strawberries. In this sensual and mysterious setting, couples who are glimpsed passing in the shadows are addressed by the dead. Traditionally death is seen by poets as something opposed to life, love, and many poets have developed the theme of *carpe diem*: enjoy the present while there is still time. The dead in Hugo's poem seem to echo this theme:

> Aimez, vous qui vivez! on a froid sous les ifs.
> Lèvre, cherche la bouche! Aimez-vous! la nuit tombe.
> (II, xxvi, 10-11, p.120)

But their message is in fact subtly different. Hugo suggests that life (and love) and death are not opposites, but complementary, part of the same overriding unity; the loves of the living and the prayers of the dead are two forms of the same human activity. The living make love, the dead pray, God can be found in both: 'Dieu veut qu'on ait aimé', and 'Dieu fait tressaillir le tombeau'; and the poem ends with an angel not opposing but mingling 'les prières des morts aux baisers des vivants'.

Four very dissimilar poems can illustrate, rather arbitrarily, the variety of Hugo's love poems. 'Le Rouet d'Omphale' (II, iii) evokes a mythical scene; 'Mon bras pressait' (II, x) seems a simple song; 'Après l'hiver' (II, xxiii) evokes a fragmentary series of scenes from nature; 'Crépuscule' (II, xxvi), one evening scene. For all their diversity, they have much in common. They all have a Hugolian use of antithesis. In its simplest form, antithesis is a contrast of ideas expressed in contrasting but parallel words; thus in 'Le Rouet d'Omphale': 'La roue agile est blanche, et la quenouille est noire'. But the whole poem is built on a series of oppositions that are antithetical in a broader sense: it consists of two halves, one light (lines 1-12), one dark (lines

13-24); one static, stating clearly what is present with a repeated 'il est', the other evoking moving presences 'qu'on ne voit qu'à demi'; one calm, reassuring (the wheel 'dort'), the other ferocious and threatening; civilized luxury set against primitive evil. The contrast is underlined on the level of syntax and vocabulary: short and simple sentences set against long and complex ones; precise description against an accumulation of affective adjectives.

This use of an antithetical structure is frequent in Hugo; it can provide the occasion for rather facile developments at times (e.g. in II, viii, or II, xviii). But its use in 'Le Rouet d'Omphale' is undeniably effective. It operates on multiple levels, and its function is not simply to contrast two terms. For Hugo, antithesis was not just a way of organizing reality, but an essential characteristic of reality itself: good and evil, soul and matter, macrocosm and microcosm. His perception of reality in terms of these oppositions can give added strength to the purely aesthetic contrasts. But both in his ideas and his sensibility, what he sought was complementarity rather than simple opposition, resolution, a sense of the relatedness or unity of opposites — as we have just seen between innocence and sensuality, between love and death. 'Le Rouet d'Omphale' evokes the legend of how Hercules, sent into slavery for a year, was sold to Omphale, queen of Lydia, who set him to women's work. Hugo relies on the reader's knowledge of the legend: the spinning-wheel stands (by metonymy) for Omphale, and Hercules is represented by the mark of his club and the monsters he overcame in his labours. The protagonists are suggestively absent (together?); the key to the poem is the relationship established between the two: the final, paradoxical subordination of the monsters to the spinning-wheel, of Hercules to Omphale, of strong to weak, of man to woman in love — a pattern we have already seen in II, x. The sculpture on the plinth in lines 5-9 offers a miniature variation on the antithesis strength/weakness and on the idea of the power of love: the god Jupiter, in the form of a white bull, carries off the helpless mortal Europa, and the homage of the 'monstrueux' ocean to Europa's toes anticipates the attitude of the cowed monsters to Omphale's spinning-wheel.

The second common characteristic is dynamism. Hugo's poems are seldom static, fixed; they are nearly always dynamic, with surprising developments; not tidily symmetrical, but capable of shifts in scale, suddenly shrinking or expanding. In II, iii the decorative carving on the plinth comes to life; the small scene opens up to show a vast ocean, which in turn shrinks in submission to Europa's delicate feet. The intimate scene between the poet and his mistress in II, x opens out to the scale of the night sky and the stars (there is a similar movement at the end of 'Le Mendiant', V, ix). Such changes of scale can correspond to a change of tone from informal to solemn, or to a movement from reality to image (as in 'Le Mendiant', again), or to a sudden imaginative transformation of reality. 'Crépuscule' is full of such shifts, from small to great:

> Le vent fait tressaillir, au milieu des javelles,
> Le brin d'herbe, et Dieu fait tressaillir le tombeau.

Then Hugo shifts back to the small-scale and realistic:

> La forme d'un toit noir dessine une chaumière;
> On entend dans les prés le pas lourd du faucheur.
>
> (II, xxvi, 21-22, p.120)

But the reassuring rustic scene of the house silhouetted in the twilight is itself abruptly changed by a single word: 'faucheur'. The homeward-plodding man becomes the traditional figure of death with his scythe, all the more sinister for being heard, not seen.

It is more difficult to generalize about Hugo's use of stanza forms. Sometimes he will exploit the possibilities of self-contained units. Each stanza of II, x pins down a separate moment, and the poem shows an ingenious progression of pronouns and possessives: 'mon bras' is in command in the first stanza; the second uses 'nous', 'nos'; in the third, 'tu' is the subject and 'me' the object. Hugo particularly likes the song-like possibilities for symmetrical repetition with variation in such three-stanza poems (see II, ii; II, iv; II, xiii). The structure of II, xxvi is very different. Although the poem consists of a series of quatrains (alexandrines with *rimes croisées*, *abab*), Hugo does not deal with separate ideas in distinct stanzas, but builds up a fluid overall movement, in keeping with the mystery and indeterminacy of the scene: nothing is seen clearly at the start. He oscillates between the notation of details, all suggesting transience, fugitivity, death: the glow-worm, the cut corn, the ripe fruit, the light of the star, and general exhortations: 'Aimez-vous!' Hugo subtly varies the form and position of the repeated injunctions:

> *Aimez, vous* qui vivez! On a froid sous les ifs.
> Lèvre, cherche la bouche! *Aimez-vous*! la nuit tombe.
>
> > (my italics)

Likewise a very symmetrical repetition at the end of the first stanza and the start of the second serves to blur the boundary between the stanzas, just as he blurs the distinction, after the fourth stanza, between the voice of the poet and the voice of the dead.

In 'Quelques mots à un autre', Hugo proclaimed: 'J'ai disloqué ce grand niais d'alexandrin' (I, xxvi, 84, p.81). This might appear to suggest both anarchic disruption for its own sake, and the lack of any alternative pattern in the 'dislocated' alexandrine. In fact, as in his attitude to poetic language, Hugo's desire is to make the rhythm appropriate to what is being expressed.[13] In 'Le Rouet d'Omphale', regularly balanced lines, each complete in itself and with a caesura after the sixth syllable, are used to evoke the calm of the atrium. These are followed by a more flexible line, with *enjambement* and displacement of the caesura, for the violent action of lines 5-9.

Hugo's 'dislocation' often consists, not just in this disruption, but in the creation of new patterns and rhythms. On the level of the line, Jacques Roubaud has noted that on the occasions when

---

[13] There are moreover limits to Hugo's dislocation of the alexandrine: the sixth syllable is always word-final and, with very few exceptions, at least equal in strength to the adjacent syllables (see Jacques Roubaud, *La Vieillesse d'Alexandre: essai sur quelques états récents du vers français*, Paris: Maspéro, 1978, pp.103-07).

Hugo uses a ternary alexandrine (4 + 4 + 4), he often underlines the new rhythm by repetitions of sound or structure, as
with the near-rhyme *niais/disloqué* in the defiant line just
quoted.[14] On the level of the stanza, the same creation of a new
rhythm can be seen in the final quatrain of II, xxiii. Hugo both
preserves the contour of the seven-syllable line by the rhymes
and the lineation, and imposes a new pattern across it,
broadening the poem out at its end, so that it might be written
thus (16 + 12):

Et nous donnons notre fièvre aux fleurs où nous
                                 appuyons nos bouches,]
Et notre lèvre sent le baiser des rayons.
                            (II, xxiii, 57-60, p.116)

The rhythm is underlined by the symmetry ('Et nous ... Et notre
...'), and serves to bring out the reciprocity of the communication of feeling: man to nature, nature to man. What is striking
is not only the sheer variety of forms in Hugo, but also the
flexibility with which he treats them: now exploiting the
possibilities of traditional constraints, now creating new
patterns and suggesting or imposing new structures across old
ones.

---

[14] *La Vieillesse d'Alexandre*, pp.105-06.

6. Grief

> 'Demeurer après l'envolement de l'ange,
> être le père orphelin de son enfant, être
> l'œil qui n'a plus la lumière ... c'est une
> sombre destinée.' (*I*, XII, p.254; Lear)

The fourth book of *Les Contemplations* has a structural role in preparing the revelations to come in Book VI, since the seer, be he Tiresias or Wotan, has traditionally to pay a price for his insight. But it strikes the reader initially as the first appearance of undeserved suffering in the life of the poet as an ordinary man. Previously he had merely observed cruelty and injustice in others' lives; now he suffers himself, and in the form of one of the clearest instances when the seemingly rational order of things is destroyed: the death of a child before its parents. The poems are however not exclusively concerned with these issues, and one can make a broad distinction between those that are essentially nostalgic recollections of 'ce passé charmant' (IV, ix) when his daughter was there, in which, as Jean Gaudon has observed, the sense of loss springs as much from the flight of time as from her death (*1*, IX, p.37), and those, very different in tone, that focus on his reactions to the sudden loss.

The poems that are principally nostalgic tend to be visual snapshots of happy moments, tinged with regret since

> Toutes ces choses sont passées
> Comme l'ombre et comme le vent! (IV, vi, 51-52, p.217)

The poet may create the impression of a loose and apparently natural, spontaneous recollection of moments in her company, often with a marked informality of rhythm. She disturbs his work:

Elle entrait, et disait: 'Bonjour, mon petit père';
Prenait ma plume, ouvrait mes livres, s'asseyait
Sur mon lit, dérangeait mes papiers, et riait,
Puis soudain s'en allait comme un oiseau qui passe.

(IV, v)

But the poem is not as artless as it might appear at first. It is not just a random collection of moments recalled, but is organized to progress from the morning (line 2), through general statements (lines 14-17), to memories associated with the evening (lines 18-21, 25-26), and to suggest that her apparent disruption of his work was also a source of revival, leaving him 'la tête un peu moins lasse', and of inspiration. In this poem, as in IV, ix, the realistic details and the natural progression through the day unobtrusively take on an added value. The dawn is both literal and metaphorical, representing youth and innocence:

Ses frères riaient ... — Aube pure!
Tout chantait sous ces frais berceaux,
Ma famille avec la nature,
Mes enfants avec les oiseaux! — (IV, ix, 17-20, p.220)

The laughter of the children is set in parallel to the birds' song, and Léopoldine herself becomes a bird: 'Moi, je n'ouvrais pas ma croisée, / De peur de la faire envoler'. At the end of the poem there is a characteristic change of tone and scale. The focus shifts from the children, laughing at the poet's gory stories, dwelt on lightheartedly, to reflective observing figures: the mother, the grandfather, and finally the poet himself, looking out of the window into the dark night sky. But the glimpse that he gets of the 'coin des cieux' also sums up a discreet chain of images applied to the children: 'astre' (line 28), 'regards du paradis' (line 36), and reinforces the link between the innocent and the celestial.

The other group of poems isolates individual moments of an emotional response to loss: despair and refusal to accept the event (IV, iv); revolt against God (IV, iii); withdrawal from society with the sense that he has done for it all that he could, or that could be expected (IV, iii; IV, xiii); resignation. Of these the most famous is 'A Villequier' (IV, xv).

The poem is a generalized meditation on the problem of apparently undeserved suffering. Hugo states his acceptance of his inexplicable loss, seeing it, like the sufferings of mankind generally, as a necessary part of a universe which only God can know entirely; he excuses his initial revolt against God, and asks for indulgence, if not for his protests, at least for his tears. He addresses God directly, speaking for himself and his loss, but also speaking for man in general (*on*, *l'homme*). What is most immediately obvious about the poem is its rhetorical side. The apostrophe to God is developed in a series of long and elaborate sentences. The first main sentence of the poem: 'Je viens à vous, Seigneur', is delayed until line 21 by a series of preceding subordinate clauses introduced by a six-times repeated 'maintenant que ...' But if there is rhetoric, the rhetorical language is being used here, not to express the sonorous and complacent confidence that Hugo is sometimes overhastily credited with, but complex and irreconcilable feelings. The very repetition of formulae like: 'Je dis que' (line 29), 'je conviens que' (lines 27, 33, 35), 'je sais que' (lines 61, 65) suggests already that the calm to which he lays claim at the start of the poem is not complete. If he were calm, and did accept his individual suffering as an inevitable part of the divine plan, would he need to insist? Is it himself that he is trying to persuade? The closer it is examined, the more it is possible to see contradictions in the poem that point to an inner conflict. Here are a few examples.

Hugo expresses confidence in providence. The world may appear unsatisfactory to us, but 'nous ne voyons jamais qu'un seul côté des choses' (line 41); God alone knows the overall pattern, 'les causes' (line 43) which could explain human suffering. But this confidence is undercut by the force and intensity with which Hugo expresses man's experience of a fragmented universe:

Tout ce qu'il voit est court, inutile et fuyant.

Vous faites revenir *toujours* la solitude
        Autour de *tous* ses pas ...

Dès qu'il possède un bien, le sort le lui retire.
Rien ne lui fut donné, dans ses rapides jours
Pour qu'il s'en puisse faire une demeure ...

(lines 44-51; my italics)

Although this is only one side of things, it is the only one man *can* see, and stanzas 10 to 14 present a totally bleak picture of human existence as insignificant and impermanent, accepted fatalistically.

There is a similar contradiction between the poet's affirmation that God is 'bon, clément, indulgent et doux' (line 26) and the presentation of human suffering in a language which suggests rather that, whatever justification He may have for His actions, it would be more reasonable to call Him the opposite (harsh, inflexible ...):

Je conviens qu'il est bon, je conviens qu'il est juste
Que mon cœur ait saigné, puisque Dieu l'a voulu!

(lines 35-36)

Hugo declares: 'Je viens à vous, Seigneur, père auquel il faut croire' (line 21). There is no doubt about Hugo's faith, but why 'il faut'? The unacceptable alternative would be to admit that the impermanent, unfair, cruel universe that Hugo characterizes here as the one we experience *is* the only reality. The contradictions of the poem are essentially between on the one hand faith — the impossibility, for Hugo, of not believing, of accepting a meaningless world as all there is — and reason, his fundamental desire for pattern and order;[15] and on the other hand, the feelings that arise from experience. The contradictions build up to stanza 30, where we reach the emotional climax to the poem on the simple conjunction *mais*:

Seigneur, je reconnais que l'homme est en délire
S'il ose murmurer;

[15] Compare section v (p.310) of 'Pleurs dans la nuit' (VI, vi), which attacks those who do not believe in God or an afterlife on the grounds that this would make the universe 'une vaste démence / Sans but et sans milieu', devoid of meaning and purpose, and with no central unity.

> Je cesse d'accuser, je cesse de maudire,
> Mais laissez-moi pleurer! (lines 117-20, p.230)

The emotion arises not just from his grief, but also from the tensions created by the conflict betweeen faith, reason, and experience.

If we find the poem moving, it is in part because Hugo has been able to generalize his feelings: he is touching on a basic dilemma, and exploring it through knowledge and echoes of a literary model. The poem highlights the same basic paradoxes as the Biblical Book of Job, in which pious and virtuous Job is visited with sufferings that he sees as unmerited and is torn between their irrationality and his sense of the magnitude of God. In both works we see the irreconcilable contradiction between man's experience of the universe as harsh and unfair, and the conviction of the goodness of God and the rationality of the world. Above all, for both Job and the poet, their sense that something is wrong in the economy of the universe is intensified by their conviction of their goodness and virtue. The idea of an afterlife, which is prominent in other poems (e.g. IV, xvii), plays a very small part in 'A Villequier': Hugo may say that death is a beginning, not the end ('Je dis que ...', lines 29-32, p.227), but this is not how it is *felt* in the poem, where his sense of loss is total, irreconcilable with an ordered universe and a benevolent deity. He talks to his daughter 'comme si ... cet ange m'écoutait' (lines 127-28, p.230): the note of loss would be lessened if he suggested that he knew she could hear him. The idea of immortality and its possible rewards and punishments is likewise foreign to the Book of Job, where we are left with an absolute of suffering for which there can be no adequate compensation.

It is not surprising to find that Job figures prominently among the books of the Bible that Hugo made fragmentary attempts to paraphrase in verse in 1846, the year that he completed the bulk of the poems in Book IV, nor that there are occasional echoes of its language in the poem.[16] More interestingly, both share a

---

[16] Compare e.g. Job 7. 17: 'Qu'est-ce que l'homme mortel, que tu en fasses un si grand cas, et que tu penses à lui?' with lines 61-62: 'Je sais bien que vous avez bien autre chose à faire / Que de nous plaindre tous ...'

common tone: both Job and Hugo talk to God directly, with a mixture of humility, affront, and self-righteousness — attempting to get God to see it *their* way. But it is not a question here of 'influence' or 'sources', nor even, as Journet and Robert have suggested, that the same misfortunes provoke the same protests (*26*, p.128); it is as if the common theme had enabled Hugo to bring into focus the fundamental paradoxes and emotions of the poem.

Some readers are tempted to react to Hugo's eloquence by suspecting his sincerity, arguing that genuine feelings are intensely individual, resist expression in a language common to all, and are silent or inarticulate.[17] But it is equally true that deep grief can try to exhaust itself in language, and is too great for utterance in few words. The length can convey the impression that words cannot encompass all his feelings, and the sudden recourse to simple language in such a context ('laissez-moi pleurer') can paradoxically highlight this inadequacy. At the end of the poem, thirteen lines of subordinate clause lead up to the movingly lame understatement:

> Considérez que c'est une chose bien triste
> De le voir qui s'en va! (lines 159-60, p.231)

There seems no doubt that Hugo did suffer as an individual; but this feeling has only biographical interest. As a *poet*, Hugo talked of loss, but, as he insisted in the preface, not just of his suffering. Rather than trying to capture its individuality, he exploits the fact that he is using a public language. He establishes a continuity with those who have talked of these things before, and also with the reader, who can structure *his* feelings with the help of Hugo's words.

The simplicity of a poet is of course just as much a deliberate and analysable use of language as is his eloquence. At the end of 'Claire P.', an episodic and rather weak poem about the death of Juliette Drouet's daughter,[18] the poet addresses the dead girl

---

[17] 'L'émotion est toujours neuve et le mot a toujours servi; de là, l'impossibilité d'exprimer l'émotion': Hugo, *Les Travailleurs de la mer (1*, XII, p.767).

[18] Which triggered off the writing of most of the poems on Léopoldine's death.

in the one moving passage of the poem:

> Claire, tu dors. Ta mère, assise sur ta fosse,
> Dit: — Le parfum des fleurs est faux, l'aurore est fausse,
> L'oiseau qui chante au bois ment, et le cygne ment,
> L'étoile n'est pas vraie au fond du firmament,
> Le ciel n'est pas le ciel et là-haut rien ne brille,
> Puisque lorsque je crie à ma fille: 'Ma fille,
> Je suis là. Lève-toi!' quelqu'un le lui défend; —
> Et que je ne puis pas réveiller mon enfant! —
> $\qquad\qquad\qquad\qquad\qquad$ (V, xiv, 63-70, p.271)

The death of the child has again overthrown the natural order
for the parent. The extent of her grief is suggested by an
enumeration: the whole world is now a lie for her. The
enumeration is built up from a series of syntactically very simple
sentences, either linked by *et* or juxtaposed; the repetitions
('faux', 'ment', 'ma fille') intensify the mood of flat despair,
and the moved caesura in lines 64 and 65 further emphasizes 'est
faux' and 'ment'. The everyday nature of what the mother says:
the simplest maternal gesture is now impossible for her, gives a
bitter twist to the cliché of death as sleep ('tu dors', line 63), and
shows Hugo's awareness, as at the end of 'A Villequier', of the
power of understatement.

   The same simplicity and understated ending characterize
'Demain, dès l'aube' (IV, xiv). The emotion is again generalized,
here implicitly: the 'tu' that the poet addresses has no specific
age, sex, or even relationship with the speaker. The poet talks to
this person as if alive; the poem opens with dawn and its
associations of beginning, departure, optimism, and the poet
seems to anticipate a rendez-vous. Gradually the mood becomes
sombre through a series of hints in the second stanza; the final
stanza brings evening and the delayed revelation that the goal is
a tomb. The poem moves progressively to the more precise,
from vague 'forêt' and 'montagne' to the place-name
'Harfleur', and closes with offerings which are effective
precisely because they are specific and enigmatic; not overtly
symbolic, but suggestive. Both are simple offerings from nature

(life continues?); the holly is evergreen (memories are kept alive?). Nevertheless if the poem is compared to 'A Villequier', I feel that it does show a simplification of experience, achieved for maximum emotional and dramatic effect, rather than an expression of the contradictions of experience. It offers a conventional image of grief blotting out the world around. This may be psychologically true, but the role that Hugo is striking here — the element of pose and even of self-pity is perhaps most intrusive in the second stanza — is one that excludes the tensions and complexities that make 'A Villequier' a more rewarding poem. There the drama is internal and the surprises arise from the tensions inherent in the theme; in 'Demain, dès l'aube' there is only dramatic movement, and an effect of surprise that arises solely from the presentation.

7. Nature

'Une force démesurée, un charme exquis.'
(*I*, XII, p.236; Shakespeare)

The response to nature in *Les Contemplations* shows two contrasting facets: one whimsical and lighthearted, the other solemn. The first brings nature to life, attributing to it human actions, desires, and intention in a mood of playfulness. The different aspects of nature are brought together in good-humoured familiarity:

> De la source, sa cuvette,
> La fleur, faisant son miroir,
> Dit: 'Bonjour', à la fauvette,
> Et dit au hibou: 'Bonsoir'. (I, xiv, 29-32, p.64)

Traditional hierarchical distinctions are broken down: birds talk, but so do the flowers, and even 'l'ornière creuse / Gronde le lourd chariot' (lines 39-40, p.64). In this poem, 'A Granville, en 1836', the poet relies on his ingenuity to devise, in each short stanza, a novel variation on the omnipresent idea of love. The ingenuity also seems to infect the rhymes ([nidil]):

> Il n'est pas de lac ni d'île
> Qui ne nous prenne au gluau,
> Qui n'improvise une idylle,
> Ou qui ne chante un duo. (lines 21-24, p.64)

In a fanciful reversal, it is the humans who are here caught like limed birds by the mood of nature.

The concentration on small aspects of nature: flowers, birds, and insects, can lead to capricious distortions of scale:

La croupe du bœuf dans l'herbe
Semble un mont dans les forêts. (lines 35-36, p.64)

Of course we know that it isn't; it is all a game, and this playfulness itself is something that Hugo occasionally projects explicitly on nature:

Le moineau d'un coup d'aile, ainsi qu'un fol esprit,
Vient taquiner le flot monstrueux qui sourit;
L'air joue avec la mouche et l'écume avec l'aigle.
(VI, x, 23-25, p.339)

To some extent this humanization represents a domestication of nature, a subordination of it to man. But Hugo's technique differs from that of a Gautier, who offers superficially similar miniaturized scenes in a series of brief stanzas. Here for instance is the latter's blackbird, dressed up like a man:

Un oiseau siffle dans les branches
Et sautille gai, plein d'espoir,
Sur les herbes, de givre blanches,
En bottes jaunes, en frac noir.[19]

Gautier is interested in the transformation of the inherently unrewarding raw material of nature by the poet's imagination, which dissolves it in a series of images. Of the seasons, he privileges winter and spring because nature then seems visually least familiar, either covered with frost and snow or repainted. Hugo's descriptions, for all their caprice, seem to communicate a mood really *in* nature: one of joy, amorousness, and harmony in I, xiv:

Les vagues font la musique
Des vers que les arbres font. (lines 59-60, p.65)

'Premier mai' (II, i) is imbued with a pervasive mood of

19 Théophile Gautier, 'Le Merle', *Emaux et camées*, Paris: Garnier, 1954, p.120.

amorous sensuality; Hugo's spring is a season when one is most aware of the rebirth of the forces of life running through all the aspects of nature. The small things that he picks out all participate in this cosmic renewal:

> Les oiseaux dans les bois, molles voix étouffées,
> Chantent des triolets et des rondeaux aux fées;
> Tout semble confier à l'ombre un doux secret;
> Tout aime, et tout l'avoue à voix basse.
>
> (II, i, 25-28, p.90)

Without interpreting literally this animation of the birds, we nevertheless sense through it something inherent in nature.

These poems in consequence do not form a separate category of poem totally different in themes and technique from the more serious nature poems, but constitute just one variant on fundamental preoccupations: the force of life and all-pervading sexuality. The poet who is the 'amoureux des fleurs' is also the contemplative 'rêveur' (I, ii). 'Le firmament est plein de la vaste clarté' encompasses both extremes, moving gradually from the small and the precise to the cosmic, from light, spring, and youth to evening. It starts with a mood of joy, gaiety, and verbal fun ('Qu'a-t-il?' meaning both: 'What is the matter with him?' and 'What has he got?'):

> Qu'a donc le papillon? qu'a donc la sauterelle?
> La sauterelle a l'herbe, et le papillon l'air;
> Et tous deux ont avril, qui rit dans le ciel clair.
>
> (I, iv, 8-10, p.36)

It progresses through solemn celebration: 'L'hosanna des forêts, des fleuves et des plaines, / S'élève gravement vers Dieu', to awe in the final contemplation of the constellations of the night sky. Literally everything, 'l'infini tout entier', comes together in a feeling both intense and imprecise ('extase') and a movement that suggests both an aspiration upwards, towards God, and the surge of a wave in which the component parts are lost:

L'infini tout entier d'extase se soulève. (line 39, p.37)

The anthropomorphic vision which was a reassuring domestication of nature on a small scale, with friendly birds and flowers
chatting to the poet, is disconcerting on this vaster scale:

Le soir vient; et le globe à son tour s'éblouit,
Devient un œil énorme et regarde la nuit.

(lines 29-30, p.37)

A simple static metaphor, such as 'le globe, cet œil qui regarde la
nuit', would be less startling; we seem to *see* the sudden transformation of the earth seen from space (an uncanny anticipation
on Hugo's part) taking place. Hugo's use of the metaphor is
strikingly dynamic. The effect is both sinister (the floating
eyeball) and unsettling. The individual is dwarfed; if the earth
shrinks to the size of an eye, what must be the size of what it is
looking at?

In two of the great nature poems of *Aujourd'hui*,
'Mugitusque boum' (V, xvii) and 'Eclaircie' (VI, x), awe in the
face of nature is clearly linked not just to its size, but to the idea
of the formless, the contourless. In 'Eclaircie' the effect is
ultimately reassuring: the title evokes the 'sunny interval' after a
shower or a storm when all is refreshed and revived. In a
moment of magical calm, opposites are reconciled and united:
sea and shore, sunlight and the dark beneath the sea, life and
death, cradle and tomb, soul and body. The sense is both of
spiritual calm, as 'la grande paix d'en haut vient comme une
marée', and also of mobility and sexuality as the mood gradually
spreads across the scene: 'baiser', 'palpite', 'frisson'. A
principle of unity, 'un immense baiser', is felt behind the
diversity of nature, which Hugo suggests here, as often, by
enumeration (lines 11, 34). And one of the forms this harmony
takes is a reconciliation between on the one hand things that are
finite and limited, and on the other the vast and formless
elements that usually pose a threat to man: between the sparrow
and the wave, between the fly and the air.

In 'Mugitusque boum' the poet hears in the lowing of the

cattle an injunction to all the aspects of nature to an intensity of life: 'Etres! choses! vivez! sans peur, sans deuil, sans nombre!'; an injunction also to fecundity and love:

> O palpitations du grand amour farouche!
> Qu'on sente le baiser de l'être illimité!
>
> > (V, xvii, 30-31, p.275)

The movement is amplified to encompass both human domesticity and a nature that is at once peaceful, mysterious, and progressively darkening. The invocation closes with an anticipation of serenity (line 32) analogous to the 'grande paix d'en haut' of 'Eclaircie'. But then the poet stands back to reflect on the message of nature, the same now as it was in the time of Virgil.[20] The implications of his reflection are clearer if we ignore the metre:

> Ainsi vous parliez, voix, grandes voix solennelles;
> et Virgile écoutait comme j'écoute,
> et l'eau voyait passer le cygne auguste,
> et le bouleau le vent,
> et le rocher l'écume,
> et le ciel sombre l'homme...
> O nature! abîme! immensité de l'ombre!

We have here a series of antitheses between things that are individually distinct and larger entities that are formless, continuous wholes without contours. The opposition works on four separate levels: animal, vegetable, mineral, then human: swan/water, birch/wind, rock/foam, man/sky. The device known as chiasmus disguises the symmetry: instead of repeating the pattern *ab ab*, Hugo reverses it the second time to provide variety: *ab ba*. The antitheses culminate in an exclamation of awe mingled with terror at the implied contrast between the transitory and finite individual and eternal nature, dark and

---

[20] The title of the poem, translated in the opening words, is a quotation from the *Georgics*, his poem on husbandry, and several lines of the poem echo lines from the Latin poet (see *26*, pp.152-53), notably lines 10-11 and 13.

unfathomable. A similar, more anguished contrast between the consciousness of the individual and the serene self-sufficiency of nature recurs in 'Paroles sur la dune' (V, xiii). This opposition between the finite and the formless is a fundamental one in Hugo's imagination, and as much as the contrast between small and vast, or weak and strong,[21] is often basic to the structure of the poems.

The image that Hugo presents of nature in these poems remains very generalized, even in those that explicitly evoke the Channel Islands, such as V, xiii, commemorating two years of exile in Jersey, or V, xxiv, located on the island of Sark. If on occasion he names individual trees, birds, or flowers (e.g. V, xxiii, 8-11, p.281), he can equally often be content with *oiseau*, *arbre*, *fleur*. In general the degree of precision corresponds to its appropriateness in context, specificity of flowers or birds tending to accompany lighter moments. Even when Hugo seems to evoke a particular scene as observed in a given moment, it does not compose a coherent visualizable picture. 'Lettre' (II, vi) starts: 'Tu vois cela d'ici', and builds up a series of spatial indications: 'à droite' (line 8), 'voilà les premiers plans' (line 10), 'devant moi' (line 16); but even here, the poem is held together, not as a picture, but thematically. A pervasive opposition runs through the proliferation of details observed: between the vast sea on the one hand (lines 7, 16-17, 24, 36-44) and the 'tranquille village' on the other. Old roofs, old chapel, twisted elms, rusty cart, patois, a patriarchal rope-maker ... all these are small-scale and reassuringly traditional, as opposed to the departure and adventure evoked by the sea.

This reliance on thematic coherence is evident in poems like 'Mugitusque boum' and 'Eclaircie', where the idea of the current running through nature is itself the theme running through the poem. The life in nature is always intense, exuberant; there are no half-measures: 'Prés, emplissez-vous d'herbes!' (V, xvii, 5, p.274). It is often very clearly sexualized, both in the impudent shamelessness of nature in the fanciful poems, and in the solemnity of 'Eclaircie'. In this poem we find

---

[21] Baudelaire noted Hugo's fascination with strength and his corresponding movement of pity towards the weak (*31*, p.738).

not only the overt 'immense baiser' of the shore and the sea, but
also the following lines:

> L'être, éteignant dans l'ombre et l'extase ses fièvres,
> Ouvrant ses flancs, ses seins, ses yeux, ses cœurs épars,
> Dans ses pores profonds reçoit de toutes parts
> La pénétration de la sève sacrée. (VI, x, 10-13, p.339)[22]

The description initially seems to suggest something human,
receptive ('ouvrant'), and female, but the subsequent
enumeration of nouns slides into an evocation of something
unimaginable, vast, one and yet multiple, which seems to stand
for all physical life. The final line presents a very Hugolian
linking of a word evoking human sexuality with both the vegetal
(sap) and the divine.

It is natural that this sense of life in all aspects of nature
should abolish hierarchies and distinctions between the
traditional realms. All can be set in parallel, sometimes conventionally, as when nests are set alongside houses (V, xvii, 23),
sometimes more strikingly: 'Vis, bête; vis, caillou; vis, homme;
vis, buisson!' (V, xvii, 8). This blurring of traditional categories
is reinforced by Hugo's use of metaphors to transform the
objects of the real world, whimsically humanizing birds, trees,
and flowers, or turning a headland into a shepherd and the white
wavecrests beneath it into sheep (V, xxiii). This last transformation is helped by the fact that our maritime 'white horses'
are 'moutons' in French. Elsewhere the starting-point for the
metaphor is not a traditional verbal association, but a visual
analogy:

> Les pins sur les étangs dressent leur verte ombelle.
>
> (I, iv, 19, p.37)

One thinks of the tall trunk leading up to the outspreading top
branches characteristic of the Scots Pine and its similarity to the
flower-cluster of an umbelliferous plant like cow-parsley; the
analogy was sufficiently novel for Hugo to have to struggle to

[22] The Collection Poésie edition has the misprint 'reins' for 'seins' in line 11.

prevent the printers 'correcting' the final word to 'ombrelle' (*4*, I, p.29). If, in 'Crépuscule', the everyday could be transformed into the mythical (the returning reaper in the twilight into Death), the converse happens when the fresh light of 'Eclaircie' evokes dawn and its sounds:

> Le premier pas du vent, du travail, de l'amour,
> De l'homme, et le verrou de la porte sonore,
> Et le hennissement du blanc cheval aurore.
>
> (VI, x, 20-22)

The mythical horse that drew the sun-god's chariot across the sky has become realistic, and fitted into a vivid scene where we hear the farmer start his day's work, unbolt the stable door ...

'Le blanc cheval aurore' is an instance of a device for presenting an image that has been termed *métaphore maxima*.[23] It can be seen as a striking extension of the use of a metaphorical noun in apposition:

> Les constellations, ces hydres étoilées. (I, iv, 35, p.37)

Hugo's suppression of any barrier, *comme* or comma, between the two nouns serves to create out of the two terms a single unit — one is tempted to say, a single being, particularly when the metaphorical noun comes first, not second, and the metaphor is sustained in the subsequent sentence, e.g. by a verb:

> Je regarde ...
> S'envoler, sous le bec du vautour aquilon,
>   Toute la toison des nuées. (V, xiii, 13-16, p.267)

> Le pâtre promontoire au chapeau de nuées,
> S'accoude et rêve au bruit de tous les infinis.
>
> (V, xxiii, 40-41, p.282)

In many of these poems on nature, the movement is as free as in the 'Réponse' (I, vii). Held together by a simple antithetical

---

[23] For a fuller discussion of its origin and use, see *8*, p.145.

structure, as in 'Pasteurs et troupeaux' (V, xxiii), or by a frame, as in 'Mugitusque boum' (V, xvii), the sequence of alexandrines in *rimes plates* often develops a theme, expanding it with a proliferation of material that gradually becomes more meaningful and leads up to a climax. The frame of 'Mugitusque boum' contains a speech that the poet hears in the lowing of the cattle. (Hugo is here adapting the rhetorical device of prosopopoeia: making someone absent or dead or something non-human speak,[24] and is using the cattle as a mouthpiece for the message that nature offers to man to interpret.) In this freely developed exhortation, short injunctions ('Vivez! Croissez!') alternate with long sentences within which enumerations hold in suspense the progress of the syntax:

Qu'on sente frissonner *dans toute la nature,*
Sous la feuille des nids, au seuil blanc des maisons,
Dans l'obscur tremblement des profonds horizons,
Un vaste emportement d'aimer, *dans l'herbe verte,*
Dans l'antre, dans l'étang, dans la clairière ouverte,
D'aimer *sans fin, d'aimer toujours, d'aimer encor,*
Sous la sérénité des sombres astres d'or!

                                        (V, xvii, 22-28, p.274; my italics)

The onward movement is constantly expected and repeatedly delayed, as series of nouns and images swim past. As Jean Gaudon has noted (*12*, p.407), we are at the opposite pole from Classical qualities of balance, symmetry, restraint; the whole form of the poem, from overall structure to syntax, suggests both the richness and variety of life, and also its underlying unity and coherence. Rhythm plays a crucial part in this creation of life and movement. In a sequence of alexandrines with *rimes plates*, our expectation is for the main pauses to occur at the end of each couplet, each line, each half-line. In the final section of this poem, Hugo sustains onward momentum by delaying the satisfaction of this expectation, while creating across the alex-

---

[24] The many voices that the poet hears can be seen as variations on the figure, notably the voices from nature (e.g. the bird of III, viii) and from apparitions (e.g. VI, iii).

andrine new and complex patterns. The final five lines could be redistributed (see above, p.62) as an alexandrine, followed by two ten-syllable lines, three six-syllable lines, and a final eleven-syllable one. The effect of the ever shorter segments is to accelerate the movement down to 'l'homme', emphasized and isolated at the start of the last alexandrine. Then, after two slow exclamations: 'O nature! abîme!', the six syllables of 'immensité de l'ombre' bring us back to the regular hemistich (half-line) of the alexandrine in a rhythm of 4 + 2 that exactly echoes the start of the first line of the poem: 'Mugissement des bœufs'. The sustained non-coincidence of syntactical units with the pattern of the rhyme-scheme and the lineation is resolved in a final delayed concord as the two finish together. The effect, as we saw with the syntax, is of forward movement, suspense, final resolution, making the rhythm an effective vehicle for a vision of nature that stresses mobility, diversity, and tensions finally resolved in harmonious unity.

8. Visions

'Ses métaphores sortent de l'éternité,
éperdues; sa poésie a un profond sourire
de démence; la réverbération de Jéhovah
est dans l'œil de cet homme. C'est le sublime en plein égarement. Les hommes ne
le comprennent pas, le dédaignent et en
rient.' (*I*, XII, p.181; St John the Divine)

The visionary poems in Book VI form the climax of the volume:
the final stage of the poet's evolution after the process of liber-
ation, discovery, and isolation traced in the previous sections.
The poems alternate, with a Hugolian polarity, between those
that express a thrusting optimism in the power of the mind to
force the ultimate secrets (the bold assertions and confident
future tenses of 'Ibo'), in the poet's power to change the world
('Les Mages'), and moments of doubt (VI, iii), uncertainty
('Horror', VI, xvi), and terror (VI, xiv).

'Ce que dit la bouche d'ombre' (VI, xxvi) provides, in the
form of the monologue of 'le spectre', the fullest exposition of
Hugo's beliefs. In traditional terms, it is a theodicy: a vindication of divine providence in view of the existence of evil in the
world. But although it exposes a theory, it is, like the 'Réponse à
un acte d'accusation', intensely dramatic in its use of monologue, in turn abrupt and loquacious; in its surprises; above all,
in its representation of the issues in visual and tangible form.
The terms that come to mind most readily to characterize some
sections, notably those depicting the punishment of criminals
after their death, are verve and glee.

The essential ideas could be expressed in terms of a few simple
points. To be distinct from God, who is perfection, creation was
necessarily imperfect, and so contained evil. The form evil took
was matter; the material world is a fallen world. All creation can
be seen as a continuous ladder, rising from the mineral through

the vegetable to the animal and man, 'le milieu' (line 392, p.398): this suggests both man's intermediate status, and also his centrality in Hugo's view of creation. Above man come 'esprits purs' and angels, and then God (line 162, p.391). Man has freedom of action; his virtuous or vicious actions are rewarded after death by promotion or demotion on the ladder. Souls reincarnated further down have no freedom, but, unlike man, know their past life; aware of their sins, of being cut off from God, they can do nothing about it and suffer in expiation. This suffering provokes God's pity and forgiveness, and the poem closes with the hope of a reunion of creation with the Creator.

Recent critics have stressed that these ideas are by no means peculiar to Hugo. Robert and Journet have shown how they can be linked with traditional ideas: that of the necessary imperfection of creation goes back at least to St Augustine (*26*, p.218), and Hugo himself noted about what the table-rapping séances in Jersey had unveiled: 'une partie de cette révélation est déjà depuis des siècles dans la tradition humaine' (*1*, IX, p.1440). On the other hand, in the case of metempsychosis and the part played in it by astral migrations of souls, the ideas can be linked with other heterodox and anti-rationalist systems of his own time, and Viatte has shown how they can be seen as part of a general, and fashionable, climate (*22, passim*). What is more important than the sources of the ideas is what they can offer as themes for poetry; all critics agree that we do not have to interpret them literally for them to say something to us.

The idea of the punitive reincarnation of the criminal in a different form provides the starting-point for what is in effect a chain of metaphors. 'Verrès, / Qui fut loup sous la pourpre, est loup dans les forêts' (lines 621-22, p.404) indicates that what lies behind the idea of Verres's rebirth as a real wolf is a conventional metaphor which conveys his wolf-like rapacity as governor of Sicily. As we have seen, metaphor for Hugo is not just a suggestion of common features between two things, but a transformation of one into the other. The use of the form of the *métaphore maxima* shows the link between these metempsychoses and his images generally, when instead of saying that Atreus is like a hyena (simile), or that Tamerlane is a jackal (metaphor), he refers to 'l'hyène Atrée et le chacal Timour' (line 670, p.406). We accept these transformations in part on the basis of similarity: here, the conventional equivalence of moral turpitude and the associations of the animals. But other factors can reinforce their aptness. The sound of a single word echoes the villain's name in: 'L'*orfraie* au fond de l'ombre a les yeux de *Jeffryes*' (line 272, p.394); sometimes the effect is more subtle, as when the sounds strengthen the identification of the passive emperor Claudius with seaweed: '*Claude* est l'*algue que l'eau t*raîne de havre en havre' (line 283, p.395; my italics). We do not interpret these metamorphoses in a narrowly literal sense, any more than we do a metaphor; we do not have to accept Hugo's doctrine literally to be struck by the vividness, the aptness, and the strange specificity of the equivalences he asserts.

The idea of metempsychosis moreover plays on our feelings about the world about us. One consequence of the doctrine that Hugo stresses at the start of the poem is that 'tout est plein d'âmes', that all the objects of the material world are consciously alive. This belief would no doubt offer to Hugo as a writer an encouragement and a justification for presenting nature as alive; conversely, it is clearly *because* he tends to imagine nature in this way that the doctrine seems the more plausible to him. But both these remarks concern Hugo's motives as a writer. From our point of view, as readers, the doctrine renews and intensifies the conventional association between guilt and being watched:

> Homme! autour de toi la création rêve.
> Mille êtres inconnus t'entourent dans ton mur.
> Tu vas, tu viens, tu dors sous leur regard obscur,
> Et tu ne les sens pas vivre autour de ta vie...
> Ce que tu nommes chose, objet, nature morte,
> Sait, pense, écoute, entend. Le verrou de ta porte
> Voit arriver ta faute et voudrait se fermer...
> Dans les mauvais desseins quand, rêveur, tu te plonges,
> La cendre dit au fond de l'âtre sépulcral:
> Regarde-moi; je suis ce qui reste du mal.

> (lines 444-58, pp.399-400)

The eyes that spy on the individual in his culpable designs are those of souls punished for *their* culpable actions; they both want to stop our crimes, and are helpless to do so (a position not unlike that of the spectator of a horror-film). Hugo makes us identify with the hidden watcher: we see its thoughts and feelings, which the observed man is ignorant of, as if observing ourselves from the outside. Hugo does not just say that things are alive, but persuades us to participate in their emotions. In his doctrine, they are souls being punished by their guilty memory of their crimes: 'la mémoire est la peine' (line 588, p.403); but he makes us feel their suffering as a physical one as much as a moral one, the torture of a helpless body:

> Oh! quels yeux fixes ouverts
> Dans les cailloux profonds, oubliettes des âmes!
> C'est une âme que l'eau scie en ses froides lames;
> C'est une âme que fait ruisseler le pressoir.
>
> (lines 654-57, p.405)

What on one level is a doctrine explaining the economy of crime and punishment in creation becomes, through the presentation of the physical world in the poem, a means of awakening in us the emotions of shame, guilt, terror, pity that give the doctrine a human dimension, something that we can feel part of rather than understand or criticize rationally.

Hugo's response to something that could be treated as a scientific problem is indicative of the way that the poems play on our feelings rather than our reason. The central issue of 'A la fenêtre, pendant la nuit' (VI, ix) could be stated thus: were the universe and the heavens created once and for all, or is creation still going on? Expressed this way, the question could be linked to what was quite recently a scientific issue: 'big bang' versus continuous creation. Hugo was certainly curious about scientific discoveries, and was particularly interested in astronomy: seeing the moon from the Paris Observatory in 1834 made a lasting impression on him, and his library in Guernsey has several books on the subject. But in the poem Hugo sets up an opposition in the first section between the unstable world and the apparently fixed stars, and uses this as a starting-point for a series of what Baudelaire termed poetic *conjectures* that fall outside the domain of science (*31*, pp.740-41). Will the stars remain fixed (section ii)? How could we know the limits of God's power (section iii)? Perhaps new stars will appear (section iv)... Each conjecture arouses emotions in the face of the heavens: expectant wonder at the majesty of the universe (ii) and its proliferating life (iii), terror and fear at its fluidity (i) and unpredictability (iv), scorn for puny man's arrogance (iii).

Fears pervade many of the visionary poems; but they are not morbid or individual ones. Hugo's obsessive fears would have no power unless we shared them, and unless he embodied them in images which evoked them for us. Sometimes the basic, instinctive nature of the fear is obvious: fear of the dark, for instance. Unknown presences lurk there: 'On dirait parfois que les ténèbres, / O terreur! sont pleines de pas' ('Horror', VI, xvi, 56-57, p.350). It can make even a familiar landscape uncanny:

> Le soir vient; l'horizon s'emplit d'inquiétude...
> Le paysage obscur prend les veines des marbres;
> Ces hydres que, le jour, on appelle des arbres,
>   Se tordent dans la nuit. (VI, vi, 361-66, p.318)

Hugo also frequently plays on the fear of being imprisoned: 'Nous sommes au cachot; la porte est inflexible' (VI, vi, 31, p.307). A large part of the horror of 'Ce que dit la bouche d'ombre' springs from the idea of the punished souls of the wicked being trapped, helpless, in a new form: 'la matière leur met la chemise de force' (VI, xxvi, 276, p.394). This can take the extreme form of the fear of petrification, which metempsychosis makes possible, as the criminal can be reborn as a stone, while at the same time being conscious:

> Homme et roche, exister, noir dans l'ombre vivante!
> Songer, pétrifié dans sa propre épouvante!
>   (VI, vi, 199-200, p.313)

This fear of paralysis is clearly related to that other extreme expression of claustrophobia, the dread of premature burial,[25] which is explicitly enacted in section xi of 'Pleurs dans la nuit'. For the first five stanzas we merely watch the burial; in the last five, we are inside the coffin, and the verbs of perception make us identify with the dead man, immobile, but still aware: 'il sent', 'il a froid', 'il entend' — but in the dark, he cannot see (VI, vi, 367-78, pp.318-19). As if this were not enough, Hugo develops the further fears of the bound and helpless body being violated:

> Il est l'être vaincu dont s'empare la chose;
> Il sent un doigt obscur, sous sa paupière close,
>   Lui retirer son œil. (VI, vi, 376-78, p.319)

The same dread reappears with a different twist in 'Ce que dit la bouche d'ombre', where the punished soul is not just trapped in matter, but presented in the course of being swallowed up by it, 'presque engloutie': 'et la fleur implacable et féroce la mord' (VI, xxvi, 368-70, p.397). The implacability and ferocity attributed to the conventionally innocuous flower are, logically, characteristics of the punishment — in other words, of the economy of the universe. The horror of the image enables us to feel the nightmarish quality of this vision of life.

It is notable that in spite of the optimism of the explicit messages of poems like 'Ce que dit la bouche d'ombre' and 'Pleurs dans la nuit', what stays in the reader's mind, and what wins him over to sharing Hugo's vision, is the appeal to primitive fears. The word implies no criticism: for Hugo, 'le poëte primitif [est] en communication intime avec l'homme et la nature' (*I*, XII, p.420). Equally crucial in conveying Hugo's vision and feelings is the imagery of these poems. They are often explicitly concerned with the process of transformation, most obviously the transformation after death. The body in 'Cadaver' is absorbed back into the natural world, and can say: 'Je vais être oiseau, vent, cri des eaux, bruit des cieux ...' (VI, xiii, 23,

---

[25] Compare the discussion of the same fears in a different medium in S.S. Prawer, *Caligari's Children: the film as tale of terror*, Oxford: University Press, 1980, p.77.

p.342); we have seen how metempsychosis transforms the soul into particular creatures and things. If, as I have argued, it functions like a metaphor, imagery, and notably what Riffaterre has termed Hugo's 'métaphore en mouvement' (*37*, p.235), becomes another aspect of the process of transformation. The vast and cosmic are turned, strikingly, into the concrete and everyday; the conventional image of death as a door is renewed when we seem to touch it: 'Et que je te sens froide en te touchant, ô mort, / Noir verrou de la porte humaine!' (V, xiii, 47-48, p.268). The defiant poet, facing the unknown, turns the 'noirs éclairs' that guard it into a pack of hounds, and himself into a lion: 'Et si vous aboyez, tonnerres, / Je rugirai' (VI, ii, 127-32, p.302).

I have already noted Hugo's way of conducting an abstract argument, metrical or metaphysical, in terms of concrete imagery. The starting-point can be conventional. If life is a journey, for instance, doubt becomes a shelter on the way:

> Le Doute...
> S'offre à nous, morne abri, dans nos marches sans
> nombre,]
> Nous dit: — Es-tu las? Viens! — Et l'homme dort à
> l'ombre]
> De ce mancenillier. (VI, vi, 13-18, p.307)

The image develops with increasing precision and autonomy, but we can still identify, using I.A. Richards's terms, a 'vehicle': the poisonous South-American tree whose shade was thought to be fatal; the 'tenor', the idea conveyed by it: scepticism; and an implicit 'ground': both are deceptive and destructive shelters. In the preceding stanza we can again identify the tenor: reverie infected by doubt, but the vehicle is a vast, unimaginable, predominantly liquid landscape whose associations of heaviness, stagnation, and disease form the ground, an emotional charge which it is difficult to describe in abstract terms:

> Mon esprit, qui du doute a senti la piqûre,
> Habite, âpre songeur, la rêverie obscure

> Aux flots plombés et bleus,
> Lac hideux où l'horreur tord ses bras, pâle nymphe,
> Et qui fait boire une eau morte comme la lymphe
> Aux rochers scrofuleux. (VI, vi, 7-12, pp.306-07)

If death and the unknown frequently provoke images like this in Hugo, they provide the reader with a concrete and coherent[26] world of things to see, hear, and feel: oceans, gulfs, pits, walls, eyes, passing footsteps, all usually active, moving, and with a strong emotional charge. Behind them seem to lie truths to which we cannot have any access, other than metaphorical. In this same poem, a coffin is carried to the grave:

> Ils le portent à l'ombre, au silence, à la terre;
> Ils le portent au calme obscur, à l'aube austère,
> A la brume sans bords,
> Au mystère qui tord ses anneaux sous des voiles,
> Au serpent inconnu qui lèche les étoiles
> Et qui baise les morts! (VI, vi, 91-96, p.309)

The image is both precise (kissing) and blurred (mist, veils); both familiar (death is a new beginning, so a 'dawn'; we know about serpents from the Bible and from our primordial fears) and unimaginable (licking stars?); it has a 'rightness' which persuades us that this *is* the unknown. But the variants from Hugo's manuscript can cure us of any illusion that he simply 'saw' the unknown like this: the second and third lines were previously:

> A l'énigme; peut-être à l'espérance austère,
> Et peut-être au remords,

and a series of alternatives were tried out for 'au remords': 'au sommeil', 'aux profondeurs', 'aux abîmes', 'aux ténèbres' (*2*, II, p.1611).

The most obvious characteristic of the visionary poems, for instance of 'Pleurs dans la nuit' (VI, vi, from which all the

---

26 The images can be 'classified' (see *12*, pp.279-403) in the same way as those of his *fantaisie* (*9*, Vol. III).

following examples are taken), is the frequent, even obsessive use of certain favourite affective adjectives such as *sinistre, obscur, sombre, formidable, farouche, lugubre, noir,* and of similar forceful and ill-defined nouns, like *abîme, gouffre, puits, ténèbres, nuit.* The argument implied in the 'Réponse à un acte d'accusation' (I, vii) is most relevant here: what is important is not just the words or devices used, but how they are used, whether they are eccentric extravagance and gratuitous exaggeration, or expressive. The most crucial factor is context. The combination of a vague adjective with a precise noun can be forceful: 'Il sent un *doigt obscur*, sous sa paupière close, / Lui retirer son œil' (VI, vi, 377-78, p.319; my italics). It can be strikingly paradoxical, as when Hugo evokes the grass that grows over ruins and graves:

> La vie autour de vous croule comme un vieux cloître;
> Et *l'herbe* est *formidable*...
>
> (lines 658-59, p.328; my italics)

As Journet and Robert have argued (*26*, pp.23-26), these combinations can serve to create a new vision of the world. Just as Hugo's portrayal of nature abolished the hierarchies between the traditional realms, so too combinations of subject and verb can break down our normal distinctions between what is inanimate and what is animate: 'Il est l'être vaincu dont s'empare la chose' (line 376, p.319) strikingly gives the anonymous and inert an active grasp; 'Le mort est seul. Il sent la nuit qui le dévore' (line 367, p.318) makes the formless night some sort of beast. Distinctions are dissolved between the abstract and the concrete: 'L'immensité ricane et la tombe grimace' (line 562, p.325); 'Le problème muet gonfle la mer sonore' (line 637, p.327). The visionary world is made real and tangible; the material world is charged with life and meaning:

> Le cadavre, lié de bandelettes blanches,
> Grelotte, et dans sa bière entend les quatre planches
> Qui lui parlent tout bas. (lines 382-84, p.319)

Certain techniques of Hugo can be classified as traditional rhetorical devices. This is prosopopoeia again; we find hypallage (the transferring of an adjective that properly applies to one word, to another) in: 'Il sent la chevelure *affreuse* des racines / Entrer dans son cercueil' (lines 374-75, p.319; my italics), where it is the sensation rather than the root-growth that is horrible. But these techniques are not merely ornamental devices for making a preexisting idea more interesting; they are the means for creating a certain vision of things.

The context in which Hugo's words appear is also, in a wider sense, the volume as a whole.[27] In the same way that images which recur throughout the volume acquire particular significance, such as the eye, the formless sea, the guiding star, so too does a word like *noir*, which is already Hugolian with its strong visual effect and the possibilities it offers for antithetical contrasts with *blanc*. It occurs thirteen times in VI, vi. Hugo does not give it a purely private sense, but exploits its traditional moral associations: sorrow, mourning, perfidy, threat. Thus we find '[le] noir gibet misère' (line 152, p.311);

Nous passons, noir essaim, foule de deuil vêtue,
    Comme le bruit d'un char. (lines 77-78, p.309)

...des pleurs, gouttes farouches,
    Tombent du noir plafond. (lines 551-52, p.324)

To develop these associations at the expense of the normal visual value can lead to striking paradoxical effects. *Noir* is not only the colour of monsters and villains (II, iii); in III, xxviii, Shakespeare is compared to 'le noir lion des jongles'; the unknown of 'Ibo' is guarded by 'noirs éclairs' (VI, ii, 128, p.302); and in 'Ce que dit la bouche d'ombre' we see at the bottom of the ladder of creation, as the antipode to the radiance of God at the top,

Un affreux soleil noir d'où rayonne la nuit!
                    (VI, xxvi, 186, p.391)

[27] The index to the vocabulary of *Les Contemplations* provided by Journet and Robert is an invaluable guide in such explorations (*26*, pp.245-391).

This image has several literary antecedents,[28] but is still intensely Hugolian. It is strikingly visual and dynamic, and reinforced by a favourite affective adjective; the sinister effect of the paradoxical reversal of the usual (black sun) is intensified by the unimaginable (radiant night); and what we think of as something precise (a disk) gives way to an all-enveloping loss of contour.

---

[28] Notably Revelation 6. 12, the German writer Jean-Paul, Gautier, and Nerval's 'le *Soleil noir* de la *Mélancholie*' ('El Desdichado'); see Hélène Tuzet, 'L'Image du soleil noir', *Revue des Sciences Humaines*, 22 (1957), 479-502, and Journet and Robert, *26*, pp.228-29.

Conclusion

To seek for a single word to characterize the diversity of *Les Contemplations* is perhaps misguided, but the least unsatisfactory might be mobility. The volume unfolds a progression in the course of time from youthful iconoclasm to the confrontation with death, a fluid progression full of forward glances and retrospective echoes. It traces a movement from life to death in the course of which we become aware that these are not fixed opposites, but that death is present in life, and that the dead are amongst the living, that death will only be a beginning. It involves us in a metaphysical point of view in which mobility plays a crucial part: the individual is transformed after death, his body being absorbed into the flux of nature, his soul migrating; the universe too is involved in a movement back to God. The natural world is permeated on every level with a divine 'sève vivante', and these levels are constantly merging. The individual poems often trace an obvious movement, as in the reckless progression of 'Ibo', or take an idea and subject it to playful, gleeful or exuberant development; but even an apparently static scene, a sculpture on a plinth, an evening cliff-top scene, become mobile and dynamic. Not only the thing seen, but also scale and tone are constantly fluctuating. No poet is as skilful as Hugo in combining a firm overall syntactic framework with a fluid rhythm to maintain onward momentum. His language breaks and reforges the links between words: his imagery transforms the world before our eyes. It is a world of changing identities and dissolving contours.

Lest this be judged merely flamboyant technique, two points are worth recalling. The technique is a means to an end: it creates a world and brings it tangibly before us, and moves us by communicating human aspirations, anxieties, doubts, and fears. Secondly, one should not forget that delicacy can be as important as drama in Hugo. 'La Fête chez Thérèse' (I, xxii) is a

poem that moves from the evocation of the stylized setting of a
fête costumée, witty, precise and artificial, mingling Watteau's
fêtes galantes, eighteenth-century elegance, and Italian comedy,
to nature and the gradual invasion of an ill-defined emotion, as
the lovers go off into the falling dark beneath the trees. Hugo
subtly dissolves the boundaries between the external and the
internal worlds, and precision yields to an invasive fluidity:

> L'amante s'en alla dans l'ombre avec l'amant;
> Et, troublés comme on l'est en songe, vaguement,
> Ils sentaient par degrés se mêler à leur âme,
> A leurs discours secrets, à leurs regards de flamme,
> A leur cœur, à leurs sens, à leur molle raison,
> Le clair de lune bleu qui baignait l'horizon.
>
>   (I, xxii, 83-88, p.76)

Select Bibliography

I. EDITIONS OF HUGO'S POETRY

1. *Œuvres complètes*, ed. Jean Massin, 18 vols, Paris: Club Français du Livre, 1967-70 (*Les Contemplations* is in Vol. IX).
2. *Œuvres poétiques*, ed. Pierre Albouy, Bibliothèque de la Pléiade, 3 vols, Paris: Gallimard, 1964-74 (*Les Contemplations* is in Vol. II).
3. *Œuvres choisies*, ed. P. Moreau and J. Boudout, 2 vols, Paris: Hatier, 1950.
4. *Les Contemplations*, ed. Joseph Vianey, 3 vols, Paris: Hachette, 1922.
5. *Les Contemplations*, ed. Jacques Seebacher, 2 vols, Paris: Colin, 1964.
6. *Les Contemplations*, ed. Léon Cellier, Paris: Garnier, 1969.
7. *Les Contemplations*, ed. Pierre Albouy, Paris: Gallimard, Coll. Poésie, 1973.

II. GENERAL WORKS ON HUGO

8. Albouy, Pierre, *La Création mythologique chez Victor Hugo*, Paris: Corti, 1968.
9. Barrère, Jean-Bertrand, *La Fantaisie de Victor Hugo*, 3 vols, Paris: Corti, 1949-60.
10. ——, *Victor Hugo*, Paris, Hatier, 1952 (revised edn 1967).
11. Baudouin, Charles, *Psychanalyse de Victor Hugo*, Geneva: Mont-Blanc, 1943.
12. Gaudon, Jean, *Le Temps de la contemplation*, Paris: Flammarion, 1969.
13. Gély, Claude, *Hugo et sa fortune littéraire*, Bordeaux: Ducros, 1970.
14. Glauser, Alfred, *La Poétique de Hugo*, Paris: Nizet, 1978.
15. Gregh, Fernand, *Victor Hugo: sa vie, son œuvre*, Paris: Flammarion, 1954.
16. Guillemin, Henri, *Victor Hugo par lui-même*, Ecrivains de toujours, Paris: Seuil, 1951.
17. Juin, Hubert, *Victor Hugo*, 3 vols anticipated, Paris: Flammarion, 1980- .
18. Levaillant, Maurice, *La Crise mystique de Victor Hugo (1843-1856)*, Paris: Corti, 1954.
19. Mabilleau, Léopold, *Victor Hugo*, Paris: Hachette, 1893.
20. Maurois, André, *Olympio ou la vie de Victor Hugo*, Paris: Hachette, 1954.
21. Robert, Guy, *Chaos vaincu: quelques remarques sur l'œuvre de Victor Hugo*, 2 vols, Paris: Belles Lettres, 1976.

22.   Viatte, Auguste, *Victor Hugo et les illuminés de son temps*, Montreal: L'Arbre, 1942.

III. SPECIFIC WORKS ON LES CONTEMPLATIONS

23.   Gaillard, Pol, *'Les Contemplations': Victor Hugo*, Paris: Hatier, Coll. Profil d'une œuvre, 1981.
24.   Journet, René, and Guy Robert, *Autour des 'Contemplations'*, Paris: Belles Lettres, 1955.
25.   ——, *Le Manuscrit des 'Contemplations'*, Paris: Belles Lettres, 1956.
26.   ——, *Notes sur 'Les Contemplations'*, Paris: Belles Lettres, 1958.
27.   Lejeune, Philippe, *L'Ombre et la lumière dans 'Les Contemplations'*, Archives des Lettres Modernes, 96, Paris: Minard, 1969.
28.   Moreau, Pierre, *'Les Contemplations' ou le temps retrouvé*, Archives des Lettres Modernes, 41, Paris: Minard, 1962.
29.   Nash, Suzanne, *'Les Contemplations' of Victor Hugo: an allegory of the creative process*, Princeton: Princeton U.P., 1976.
30.   Pruner, Francis, *'Les Contemplations'*, *'pyramide-temple': ébauche pour un principe d'explication*, Archives des Lettres Modernes, 43, Paris: Minard, 1962.

IV. ARTICLES PARTICULARLY RELEVANT TO LES CONTEMPLATIONS

31.   Baudelaire, Charles, 'Victor Hugo', in *Curiosités esthétiques, L'Art romantique et autres œuvres critiques*, Paris: Garnier, 1962, pp.729-43.
32.   Bowman, Frank P., 'Lectures de Victor Hugo, "Eclaircie": new criticism, nouvelle critique, ou...', *Cahiers de l'Association Internationale des Etudes Françaises*, 23 (1971), 145-62.
33.   Clancier, Georges-Emmanuel, 'Notes sur la poétique de l'œil chez Hugo', *Cahiers du Sud*, 54 (1962), 87-96.
34.   Lechanteur, Jean, 'Les Commentaires de "Demain, dès l'aube...", de Victor Hugo', *Cahiers d'Analyse Textuelle*, 10 (1968), 117-27.
35.   Poulet, Georges, 'Hugo', in *Etudes sur le temps humain, II: la distance intérieure*, Paris: Plon, 1952, pp.194-230.
36.   Raymond, Marcel, 'Hugo mage', in *Génies de France*, Neuchâtel: La Baconnière, 1945, pp.161-89.
37.   Riffaterre, Michael, 'La Vision hallucinatoire chez Victor Hugo', *Modern Language Notes*, 78 (1963), 225-41.
38.   Seebacher, Jacques, 'Sens et structure des *Mages* (*Contemplations*, VI, 23)', *Revue des Sciences Humaines*, 28 (1963), 347-70.

CRITICAL GUIDES TO FRENCH TEXTS

edited by
Roger Little, Wolfgang van Emden, David Williams